Pocket Book on

Food Processors

Jenni Taylor

Octopus Books

Pocket Book on

Food
Processors

Jenni Taylor

Octopus Books

Contents

First published 1985 by
Octopus Books Limited
59 Grosvenor Street
London W1

© 1985 Octopus Books Limited

ISBN 0 7064 2314 3

Produced by Mandarin Publishers Ltd
22a Westlands Road, Quarry Bay,
Hong Kong

2500 **maxi**

Introduction

Food processors have certainly made their mark since they were first introduced into this country in 1974. Speed and ease of use are their strongest selling points, with versatility coming a close third.

A food processor reduces food preparation time considerably, especially for basic chores such as slicing, chopping, mincing (grinding), grating and shredding. It also enables you to produce time-consuming and elaborate recipes in a fraction of the normal time. It makes perfect pâtés and other dishes using minced (ground) meat; rich, creamy mayonnaise and hot butter sauces; creamed soups, and light pastry. It also takes the hard work out of baking – kneading bread takes seconds rather than minutes, and cakes and biscuits can be put together in almost no time at all.

This pocketbook is designed to help you make the most of your fast and efficient machine. It is not, however, intended to replace the manufacturer's instruction manual. The design, capacity and strength of the processors on the market vary considerably. Take time to check your manual before trying any recipes and techniques in this book. Some machines, for example, can only process a bread dough made from 250 g/8 oz (2 cups) flour, whilst others can process a larger quantity. Likewise, some processors can process as much as 1.75 litres/3 pints (7 cups) liquid, whilst others have a smaller capacity. It is vital you check – you may do irreparable damage.

YOUR PROCESSOR

All processors have the same basic parts: a base containing the motor; a tough acrylic or plastic bowl that locks on top of the base if the machine is direct drive, or alongside the base if the machine is belt driven; a plastic cover with a feed tube that locks on to the bowl, and a food pusher used to push the food down the feed tube on to rotating plates or blades.

Most models only operate if both the bowl and lid are locked in position – a simple but effective safety device.

The power and mode of operation varies for different models. Some machines have only one speed and are turned on by locking the lid in position or by pressing an on/off switch. Other machines, however, have a selection of speeds or a variable speed control, with the slower speeds used for some mixing and blending and the higher speeds for chopping and mincing. Full details will be given in the machine's instruction manual.

Many processing techniques call for an on/off or pulse action – the machine is turned on for a second, then off for a second – which helps prevent overprocessing. With this requirement in mind, many processors are designed with a pulse switch.

The range of plates and blades provided with the machine also varies but usually a processor is supplied with the basic SLICING, SHREDDING or GRATING plates, the versatile double-sided STEEL BLADE and a PLASTIC or NYLON BLADE. Most manufacturers offer a range of additional optional attachments.

Steel Blade

This blade has two cutting edges and is used for most processes – chopping, sifting, mincing (grinding), blending, mixing, beating and kneading. Care must be taken not to overprocess food when using this blade. Only a second's inattention and the food will be a mushy pulp!

Plastic or Nylon Blade

This blade does not have a cutting edge so is used to combine softer foods, to whip, and to make sauces, dressings and batters. Some can also be used to whisk egg whites and cream.

Slicing Plate

The thickness of the slices produced by this blade varies from model to model and also depends on the pressure exerted by the food pusher – the more pressure used to press the food down the feed tube, the thicker the slice will be. Conversely, if little or no pressure is used, the slices are likely to be paper thin. Some machines are provided with two slicing plates of different thicknesses. Use to slice fruit, vegetables, cheese and processed meats.

Shredding Plate

This plate can be used to prepare all foods that would normally be grated by hand, such as cheese, bread, vegetables, firm fruits and chocolate. Different manufacturers provide shredding plates with varying degrees of coarseness but again this can also be controlled by the amount of pressure exerted when pushing the food to be processed down the feed tube.

Chip Plate

This plate is not just for preparing chips or 'French fries'. It can also be used to chop firm fruit, chocolate and chilled fat for pastries coarsely, and to dice tomatoes.

Optional Blades, Plates and Accessories

Whisks These are specially designed for whipping cream or whisking egg whites in machines where the plastic blade does not do these tasks.

Ice Cream Maker A whisk-like blade that is used during the preparation of the ice cream mixture. It can also be used to break down ice crystals when the ice cream is semi-frozen.

Julienne Plate This is used to cut fruit and vegetables into small matchstick shapes.

Parmesan Plate A specially-designed attachment to shred very hard cheese, it can also be used for crushing ice cubes.

Ripple Disc As the name suggests, this disc produces slices of food with a rippled edge.

Citrus Juicer Used to extract juice from lemons, limes, oranges and grapefruits.

Juice Extractor Used for extracting juice from other fruits and vegetables.

Dome Cover This enables the operator to process a larger quantity of dough or pastry than normal.

Expanded Feed Tube. A tube wide enough to accommodate whole tomatoes, oranges, lemons, etc.

Feed Funnel Sit this attachment on top of the feed tube, to widen its diameter and make it easier to add dry ingredients to the feed tube.

Attachment Holder A very necessary extra which keeps the sharp plates and blades in a safe place out of the reach of children. It also helps to protect the sharp edges from being damaged and blunted.

Attachments for the Food Processor

PROCESSOR TECHNIQUES

The following tips highlight the processor's versatility and are designed to help you use your processor to the fullest.

Chopping

The steel blade will always chop food efficiently if certain steps are taken. Food to be chopped must be cut into even-sized cubes about 2 to 3 cm/1 inch. The more even the size the more evenly the processor will chop them. The smaller you cut the food, the faster the processor will cope.

Do not overload the processor. For best results, large amounts of food should be chopped in batches.

Use the on/off or pulse switch when chopping, this gives more control over the final texture because each time the machine is turned off, the food drops to the bottom of the bowl and comes in contact with the blades.

Chopping Tips
Herbs Wash and dry fresh herbs thoroughly.
Glacé Fruits Add a little of the measured flour from the recipe to the bowl when chopping glacé fruits.
Biscuit Crumbs For best results when crushing biscuits (crackers or cookies), drop them down the feed tube on to the revolving steel blade.
Hard Ingredients Nuts, the hard cheeses, such as Parmesan, and ice cubes should also be dropped down the feed tube on to the rotating blades. (Check the instruction manual to see if your processor can cope with ice cubes and Parmesan; many models cannot.)

Slicing

The secret of successful slicing is the way the feed tube is packed. For uniform slices make sure the foods stand vertically in the tube. The food also has to be packed in tightly so that as it is pushed down the feeder tube it remains in this upright position.

Cut long foods, such as carrots and cucumber, into equal lengths just slightly shorter than the feed tube. Cut foods such as beans, that are to be sliced lengthwise, just short enough to lie horizontally in the tube. Only fill the tube to about 1 cm/½ inch from the top.

Round vegetables, such as onions, potatoes, cucumbers and tomatoes, may be too large to fit the feed tube so it is best to halve them vertically before packing in the tube.

To achieve as uniform a slice as possible from foods such as lemons and tomatoes, cut a thin slice from the top and bottom so the food will remain in an upright position as it passes down the feed tube.

Foods with a tough peel, such as lemons and green peppers, should be placed in the feed tube with the skin facing towards the centre of the bowl, reducing the likelihood of the slices being torn.

Once the tube is packed correctly, turn the processor on and exert even pressure on the food pusher. The firmer the pressure, the faster the food will pass through the slicing plate and the thicker the slices will be.

Empty the processor bowl when full, and *never* let the processed foods press up against the *slicing plate*.

Slicing Tips
Cucumbers Most cucumbers are too thick to fit the feed tube, so cut in half lengthwise and scoop out the seeds with a teaspoon before processing.

Cheeses Cheddar and other medium-hard cheeses should be chilled and harder cheeses should be at room temperature. Soft cheeses, such as mozzarella, should be partly frozen before being sliced.

Meat It is possible to slice raw meat in the food processor if it is partially frozen (excellent for stir-fry dishes). *Never* attempt to slice totally frozen meat because it could damage the plates.

Hard-boiled Eggs Although these can be chopped using the steel blade, they are best sliced by hand.

Leafy Vegetables Vegetables such as spinach and lettuce can be sliced for salads. Wash and trim, then roll several leaves together before packing in the feed tube.

Cabbage Slice rather than shred cabbage for coleslaw. Simply cut out the central core, then trim the cabbage into wedges small enough to fit in the feed tube.

Mushrooms For even, uniform slices, stack the mushrooms in the feed tube on their sides.

Cutting julienne strips using the slicing plate:

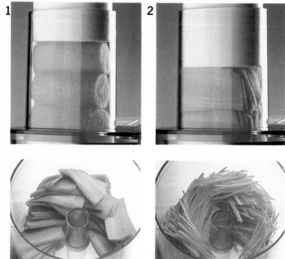

(1) Pack the feed tube lengthways with the raw vegetables and cut into slices. (2) Repack the feed tube tightly with the slices upright. Press down lightly with the pusher and cut again to form julienne strips.

Shredding

The techniques that apply to slicing also apply to shredding. Firm pressure on the food pusher gives coarse shreds and light pressure results in fine shreds. The length of the shred depends on the length of the food in the feed tube; for short shreds stack food upright and for longer shreds lay the food horizontally. (The same applies if using the julienne or chip blades.)

Kneading

A processor certainly takes the hard work out of bread making, kneading in seconds rather than the minutes it takes to knead by hand. Take care not to add too much mixture and overload the machine. Read the instruction manual to determine maximum quantities and which blade to use (in some models it is the steel blade, whilst others are equipped with a special dough blade). The process is so effortless that you can quickly prepare two small batches of dough for one large loaf.

Beating and Whisking

Food processors are excellent at beating together ingredients for batters and other soft mixtures. Unfortunately, however, few models can successfully whip cream or whisk egg whites unless they are supplied with a specially-designed whisk attachment. Check the manufacturer's manual for which blade to use.

Watch cream constantly or you could make butter!

The volume of egg whites whisked (beaten) in a food processor is not likely to be as great as if a balloon whisk or electric hand-held mixer had been used.

Mincing (grinding) Meat

The steel blade efficiently minces (grinds) meat. Trim away any bone or gristle and cut the raw meat into 2-3 cm/1 inch cubes. Place the meat in the processor bowl with the steel blade in position and, using the on/off or pulse switch, process the meat for about 5 seconds until it is minced sufficiently. Do not overprocess or it will become sticky.

Do not be tempted to mince too much meat at a time. For best results, process in 250 g/½ lb batches.

Rubbing (cutting) In

A processor is excellent for rubbing (cutting) fat into flour for pastries, scones and cakes. The machine reduces handling the mixture to a minimum, therefore a short and tender result is guaranteed.

Place the dry ingredients into the bowl, cut chilled fat into cubes, add to the bowl and process for only a few seconds, just until the mixture resembles fine breadcrumbs. Take care not to overprocess or the mixture will form a dough. Add the required liquid down the feed tube with the motor running.

Folding In

One or two stiffly beaten egg whites can swiftly be incorporated into a mixture already in the processor bowl — remove the lid, spoon the whites on to the mixture and replace the lid. Using an on/off or pulse action, process the mixture for a few seconds only until the egg whites have been combined. Do not overprocess or the air will be knocked out of the egg whites.

Flour can be folded into a cake mixture by using the same on/off technique. Again, it will only be necessary to turn the motor on and off two or three times. Overprocessing will cause a tough final product.

Creaming

Creaming fat with sugar takes only seconds and you can use butter or margarine straight from the refrigerator.

For best results, cut the fat into cubes and, using the steel blade, process until softened, then gradually add the sugar down the feed tube with the motor running. It may be necessary to stop the processor and scrape down the sides of the bowl with a spatula several times during processing.

PROCESSOR PROBLEMS

Uneven slices The feed tube has not been packed tightly enough; foods need to be arranged so they remain upright as they are pushed through the tube.

Slices too thin Insufficient pressure has been applied to the food pusher.

Torn slices of food This often happens with foods that have thick peel, such as lemons and green peppers. Always place the food in the feed tube with the peel positioned towards the inside of the bowl.

Food remaining on top of the slicing or grating plate This is quite normal. Always check that the bowl is not overfull with the food pressing against the plate.

Lumpy purées For best results, place the solid food to be puréed into the bowl with only a little of the liquid. Process until smooth, then stir the purée into the remaining liquid.

Uneven chopping This is probably caused by overloading

the bowl. Chop large quantities in batches. Remember, the smaller and more evenly chopped before processing, the more evenly chopped the processed food will be.

Cakes with poor volume This is caused by overprocessing after the flour has been added or insufficient creaming of fat and sugar. When making cakes, be sure to remove the pusher from the feed tube.

Cakes with a tough texture This is due to overprocessing once the flour has been added. Use an on/off technique when folding in the flour and process only until it has just been incorporated into the mixture.

Glutinous mashed potatoes It is very easy to overprocess potatoes, causing them to become glutinous. Follow your manufacturer's instructions, which may suggest grating cooked potato into the bowl.

Inability to grind coffee beans This is normal, as few machines grind coffee beans, peppercorns or whole spices. Check with the instruction manual.

PREPARING FOODS IN BULK

You can save even more time in the kitchen by processing certain foods in bulk, packing them in smaller quantities and refrigerating or freezing them for future use.

Herbs Chop large quantities of leafy herbs like parsley and basil and dip into them when required. The chopped herb will keep for up to a week in an air-tight container in the refrigerator and several months in the freezer.

Cheese Grate cheese for future use. This is an excellent way of using up leftover hard pieces of cheese.

Breadcrumbs Stale bread can be converted into bread-crumbs in seconds using the steel blade. For golden crumbs, toast the bread in a cool oven (140°C/275°F, Gas Mark 1) until golden, then process. Golden crumbs do not need to be refrigerated and will keep indefinitely in an airtight container.

Savoury Butters These add a touch of class to grilled (broiled) fish and meat. Place butter, garlic, fresh herbs, lemon juice or finely grated rind, or a few anchovies, into the processor and process until light and smooth. Roll into a sausage shape in greaseproof (waxed) paper, cover and freeze. Then simply slice off a little when required.

Basic Recipes

Soups

Use your processor to do the basic chopping and slicing if making old-fashioned, hearty main meal soups. A processor really comes into its own when preparing creamed hot or cold vegetable soups. For smoothest results, process the cooked vegetables with a minimal amount of the cooking liquid, then stir this smooth purée into the remaining cooking liquid.

Prawn and Pepper Chowder

Metric/Imperial	American
1 large onion, peeled	1 large onion, peeled
2 rashers bacon, rind removed	2 slices of bacon
1 clove garlic, peeled	1 clove garlic, peeled
2 tablespoons oil	2 tablespoons oil
1 large or 2 small red peppers, cored and seeded	1 large or 2 small red peppers, cored
250 g/8 oz tomatoes, skinned	½ lb tomatoes, peeled
900 ml/1½ pints chicken stock	3¾ cups chicken stock
1 tablespoon tomato purée	1 tablespoon tomato paste
1 bay leaf	1 bay leaf
1 blade of mace	1 blade of mace
25-40 g/1-1½ oz long-grain rice	2-3 tablespoons long-grain rice
1 tablespoon wine vinegar	1 tablespoons wine vinegar
salt	salt
fresh black pepper	fresh black pepper
50 g/2 oz peeled prawns	¼ cup shelled shrimp
1 parsley sprig	1 parsley sprig
8 whole prawns, to garnish	8 whole shrimp, for garnish

Using the *Steel Blade,* finely chop the onion, bacon and garlic.

Heat the oil in a saucepan and sauté the onion, bacon and garlic for about 3 minutes until soft, but not coloured.

Using the *Steel Blade,* finely chop the pepper and then

add to the saucepan and continue frying for 2 to 3 minutes, stirring constantly.

Chop the tomatoes in the processor, fitted with the *Steel Blade,* then add to the pan with the stock, purée (paste), bay leaf, mace, rice and vinegar and bring to the boil.

Add plenty of salt and pepper, cover and simmer for 35 minutes, until all ingredients are soft, stirring occasionally.

Roughly chop the prawns (shrimp) and parsley in individual batches in the processor, fitted with the *Steel Blade.* Remove the bay leaf and mace from the soup. Add the prawns (shrimp) and parsley to the pan. Taste and adjust the seasoning. Simmer for a further 5 minutes.

Serve hot in individual warmed bowls, garnished with the whole prawns. Serves 4.

Prawn and Pepper Chowder

Leek and Potato Soup

Metric/Imperial	American
500 g/1 lb leeks, cleaned	1 lb leeks, cleaned
1 onion, peeled	1 onion, peeled
50 g/2 oz butter	¼ cup butter
250 g/8 oz potatoes, peeled	½ lb potatoes, peeled
750 ml/1¼ pints chicken stock	3 cups chicken stock
salt	salt
fresh black pepper	fresh black pepper
300 ml/½ pint milk	1¼ cups milk
To garnish:	*To garnish:*
2-3 tablespoons single cream	2-3 tablespoons light cream
fresh chopped chives	fresh snipped chives

Using the *Slicing Plate,* finely slice the leeks and onion. Heat the butter in a large saucepan over moderate heat, add the leeks and onion, cover and cook gently for 10 minutes. Fit the processor with the *Chip Plate* and process the potatoes. Add to pan and cook for a further 5 minutes. Add stock, salt and pepper, cover and continue simmering for about 30 minutes. Drain; reserve the cooking liquid.

Using the *Steel Blade,* purée the vegetables, a little at a time, with a little of the cooking liquid. Stir this purée into the remaining cooking liquid and return to the rinsed out saucepan over the heat. Add the milk and bring to the boil. Adjust seasoning to taste. Serve in warmed bowls, topped with a swirl of cream and a few chives. Serves 4.
Variations:
Vichyssoise: Make Leek and Potato Soup as above, but chill thoroughly when puréed. Before serving, stir in 150 ml/¼ pint (⅔ cup) milk and almost 150 ml/¼ pint (⅔ cup) single (light) cream, reserving a little cream to add to each serving. Garnish with chives.

PÂTÉ

Smooth, creamy meat pâtés and chunky terrines can be prepared in your food processor. It can also be used to prepare a wide selection of fish and vegetable pâtés.

Farmhouse Pâté

Metric/Imperial	American
butter for greasing	butter for greasing
250g/8oz streaky bacon, rind removed	½lb sliced bacon
175g/6oz belly pork, rind and bones removed, diced	¾ cup diced fresh side pork
175g/6oz pig's liver, diced	¾ cup diced pork liver
125g/4oz chicken livers, diced	¼lb chicken livers, diced
1 onion, peeled	1 onion, peeled
1-2 cloves garlic, peeled	1-2 cloves garlic, peeled
salt	salt
fresh black pepper	fresh black pepper
½ teaspoon celery salt	½ teaspoon celery salt
2 tablespoons wine, sherry, cider or brandy	2 tablespoons wine, sherry cider or brandy
To garnish:	*For garnish:*
hard-boiled egg slices	hard-cooked egg slices
cucumber slices	cucumber slices
fresh bay leaves	fresh bay leaves

Use the butter to grease a 450g/1lb loaf tin (pan) thoroughly. Stretch about half the bacon rashers with the back of a knife and line the tin (pan) with them.

Using the *Steel Blade,* finely chop the remaining bacon with the pork, livers, onion and garlic. Add a little salt, plenty of pepper, the celery salt and the wine down the feed tube. Use the pulse or on/off switch to mix well.

Spoon the mixture into the tin (pan), pressing well into the corners, and fold the ends of the bacon over.

Place in a roasting tin (pan) containing 4cm/1½ inches water and cook in a preheated moderate oven (180°/350°F, Gas Mark 4) for 1¼ hours.

Remove from the waterbath, allow to cool slightly, then cover with a weighted plate. Leave until cold, then cover tightly and chill.

Turn out and garnish with slices of egg, cucumber and bay leaves. Serve with toast, crusty bread or crackers. Serves 6 to 8.

Smoked Fish Pâté

Metric/Imperial	American
250 g/8 oz smoked mackerel or trout fillets	½ lb smoked mackerel or trout fillets
175 g/6 oz butter, chilled and cubed	¾ cup butter, chilled and cubed
1 tablespoon lemon juice	1 tablespoon lemon juice
1 tablespoon brandy	1 tablespoon brandy
few drops of Tabasco sauce	few drops hot pepper sauce
1 clove garlic, peeled	1 clove garlic, peeled
chopped parsley to garnish	chopped parsley for garnish

Remove the skin and any bones from the fish. Using the *Steel Blade,* process all the ingredients, except the parsley, until the mixture is smooth. Transfer to a serving dish and chill. Serve garnished with chopped parsley. Serves 4.
Variation:
Peppered Pâté: Omit the Tabasco (hot pepper sauce) and instead add 2 teaspoons whole green peppercorns. If the mixture is a little too stiff, add 2 tablespoons double (heavy) cream.

MINCED MEAT

Mincing (grinding) your own meat allows you to select the best quality lean meat. Always use the on/off or pulse switch when mincing meat because it gives you a more even result.

Hamburgers

Metric/Imperial	American
500 g/1 lb lean beef, braising or rump steak, cubed	1 lb lean beef, braising or sirloin steak, cubed
1 onion, peeled	1 onion, peeled
salt	salt
fresh black pepper	fresh black pepper
butter or vegetable oil for frying	butter or vegetable oil for frying

Place half the meat and half the onion in the processor fitted with the *Steel Blade* and, using the on/off or pulse switch, process until finely minced (ground). Repeat with the remaining meat and onion. Add salt and pepper to taste.

Shape the mixture into four burgers. Heat the butter or oil in a frying pan (skillet) and fry until the burgers are tender and golden, about 7 minutes each side for braising steak, or 3 minutes each side for rump (sirloin) steak. Makes 4.

Variations:

Pepper Burgers: Add 1 tablespoon whole green peppercorns in place of the black pepper.

Cheese Burgers: Cut 50 g/2 oz Cheddar cheese into four cubes and mould a quarter of the minced mixture around each cube.

Herbed Burgers: Add 1 tablespoon chopped fresh herb of your choice or ½ teaspoon dried mixed herb.

Helpful Hint

Most of your favourite recipes can be prepared in a food processor, although the order in which you tackle the ingredients in the recipe may change. You may also find that the recipe has to be prepared in two or more batches (not the hassle it sounds when you consider how fast the food processor is). Use your processor to help with any of the basic preparation, such as mincing (grinding).

Hamburgers

Italian Meat Sauce

Metric/Imperial
125 g/4 oz button
  mushrooms
1 large onion, peeled
1 green pepper, cored and
  seeded
3 tablespoons oil
500 g/1 lb lean stewing
  beef, partially frozen
2 cloves garlic, peeled
500 g/1 lb tomatoes,
  skinned, or 1 × 410 g can
  tomatoes
2 tablespoons tomato
  purée
150 ml/¼ pint beef stock
150 ml/¼ pint dry red wine
  (optional)
2 bay leaves
2 teaspoons dried oregano
salt
fresh black pepper

American
1 cup button mushrooms
1 large onion, peeled
1 green pepper, seeded
3 tablespoons oil
1 lb lean stewing beef,
  partially frozen
2 cloves garlic, peeled
1 lb tomatoes, peeled, or
  1 × 1 lb can tomatoes
2 tablespoons tomato paste
⅓ cup beef stock
⅔ cup dry red wine
  (optional)
2 bay leaves
2 teaspoons dried oregano
salt
fresh black pepper

Using the *Slicing Plate,* slice the mushrooms and reserve. Slice the onion and pepper in individual batches. Heat the oil in a large saucepan. Add the onion and pepper and sauté gently until soft.

Using the *Steel Blade,* mince (grind) the beef and garlic in batches, using the on/off or pulse switch. Add to the saucepan and cook gently, stirring continuously, until the meat is browned.

Chop the fresh tomatoes, if using, in the processor, then add the tomatoes to the saucepan with the remaining ingredients except the mushrooms. Simmer, uncovered, for about 45 minutes, stirring occasionally.

Add the reserved mushrooms 10 minutes before the end of the cooking time. Remove the bay leaves and serve over spaghetti with a sprinkling of grated Parmesan, on rice, as a base to Shepherd's Pie or as a filling for savoury pancakes (crêpes). Serves 4 to 5.

STUFFINGS

The speed with which your processor can prepare ingredients for stuffings enables you to become far more adventurous with your flavour combinations.

Mushroom and Bacon Stuffing

Metric/Imperial	American
125 g/4 oz streaky bacon, rind removed	6 slices bacon
175 g/6 oz mushrooms	1½ cups mushrooms
25 g/1 oz butter	2 tablespoons butter
4 slices fresh brown bread	4 slices fresh brown bread
1 parsley sprig	1 parsley sprig
2 tablespoons soured cream	2 tablespoons sour cream
pinch of dried basil	pinch of dried basil
4 juniper berries, crushed (optional)	4 juniper berries, crushed (optional)
salt	salt
fresh black pepper	fresh black pepper

Using the *Steel Blade,* dice the bacon and chop the mushrooms in individual batches. Reserve.

Melt the butter in a large frying pan (skillet), add the bacon and cook gently for 4 minutes. Stir in the mushrooms and sauté for a further 4 minutes. Remove from the heat.

Using the *Steel Blade,* finely chop the bread and the parsley. Add with the remaining ingredients to the mushroom and bacon mixture. Mix well. Use to stuff a medium-sized chicken.

Helpful Hints

If you are mixing several dry ingredients with a liquid it is best to mix the dry ingredients thoroughly in the procesor bowl, then pour the liquid down the feed tube with the motor running.

The secret of a smooth purée is not to add too much liquid to the solid food in the processor bowl. Once added, the liquid cannot be taken away.

Lamb with Apricot and Almond Stuffing

Apricot and Almond Stuffing

Metric/Imperial
1 small onion, peeled
2 tablespoons vegetable oil
50 g/2 oz white bread
2 parsley sprigs
25 g/1 oz flaked almonds
1 tablespoon chopped
   fresh or 1 teaspoon dried
   marjoram
125 g/4 oz dried apricots,
   soaked in cold water for 2
   hours
a little flour
grated rind of 1 orange
1 egg, beaten
salt
fresh black pepper

American
1 small onion, peeled
2 tablespoons vegetable oil
2 slices white bread
2 parsley sprigs
¼ cup slivered almonds
1 tablespoon chopped
   fresh or 1 teaspoon dried
   marjoram
¾ cup dried apricots,
   soaked in cold water for 2
   hours
a little flour
grated rind of 1 orange
1 egg, beaten
salt
fresh black pepper

Using the *Steel Blade,* chop the onion. Heat the oil in a large saucepan, add the onion and cook until soft. Remove and cool. Place the bread, parsley, almonds and marjoram in the processor and process until crumbs form and the herbs are well chopped. Stir into the onion mixture. Drain the apricots and place in the processor with a little flour. Chop roughly, then add to the mixture with the orange rind, egg, salt and pepper. Mix well and use to stuff a 2 kg/4½ lb shoulder of lamb or a piece of boned veal.

SAUCES

A food processor makes a perfect hot or cold emulsified sauce every time – no more curdling, no more thin sauces and usually the longer you process a Mayonnaise or a Hollandaise Sauce, the thicker it will become.

Use your processor to beat away the lumps in traditional white sauce and to purée well-seasoned, cooked vegetables to give a healthy, fat and flour free sauce.

Mayonnaise

Metric/Imperial	*American*
2 eggs	2 eggs
1 tablespoon vinegar	1 tablespoon vinegar
1 clove garlic, peeled	1 clove garlic, peeled
1 teaspoon mustard powder	1 teaspoon mustard powder
salt	salt
fresh black pepper	fresh black pepper
300 ml/½ pint olive oil	1¼ cups olive oil

Using the *Steel Blade,* process the eggs, vinegar, garlic, mustard and salt and pepper to taste until well blended.

With the motor still running, slowly pour the oil down the feed tube in a steady stream. Process for about 1 minute until the mayonnaise is thick and creamy. Makes about 350 ml/12 fl oz (1½ cups).

DON'T remove the blade before emptying the bowl. Instead, hold the blade in place with a finger whilst you pour out the contents.

Processor Cream

Metric/Imperial	American
125 g/4 oz unsalted butter	½ cup sweet butter
150 ml/¼ pint milk	⅔ cup milk
1 teaspoon gelatine	1 teaspoon gelatine
1 to 2 drops vanilla essence	1 to 2 drops vanilla
½ teaspoon sugar	½ teaspoon sugar
(optional)	(optional)

Place the butter, milk and gelatine in a small saucepan over moderate heat and heat very gently, stirring frequently, until the butter has melted. Do not boil the mixture or the flavour will be impaired. Add the vanilla and sugar, if using. Place the mixture in the food processor fitted with the *Steel Blade* and process at top speed for 30 seconds. Pour into a bowl, cover and refrigerate for at least 3 hours. The cream may now be whipped, ready for use. If the cream is too thick, add a little milk. Makes 300 ml/½ pint (1¼ cups).

Variation:

Single (light) cream: Use only 75 g/3 oz (6 tablespoons) unsalted (sweet) butter and proceed as above.

BATTERS

Use your processor to prepare pancakes (crêpes) and fritter batters. They are guaranteed to be lump-free.

Basic Batter

Metric/Imperial	American
125 g/4 oz plain flour	1 cup all-purpose flour
pinch of salt	pinch of salt
1 egg	1 egg
300 ml/½ pint milk	1¼ cups milk

Using the *Steel Blade*, process all the ingredients until smooth. Leave to stand for 15 minutes before using, adding a little more milk if necessary. Alternatively, use immediately for pancakes (crêpes), or Yorkshire Pudding. Makes 600 ml/1 pint (2½ cups).

Variations:
Coating Batter: Halve the quantity of liquid in the recipe.
Dessert Crêpes: Add another egg, 2 tablespoons sugar and 2 tablespoons melted butter. Makes about 20 crêpes.

PASTRIES

A food processor is a boon for those who have never mastered the art of making pastry. It takes the hard work out of rubbing (cutting) fat into the flour for short pastries, and the chip plate can be used to dice fat for rough puff or soda pastry. Whichever recipe you use, the result will always be a perfect pastry.

Shortcrust Pastry (Basic Pie Dough)

Metric/Imperial	*American*
350 g/12 oz plain flour	¾ lb all-purpose flour
175 g/6 oz fat (half lard, half butter)	¾ cup shortening
	pinch of salt
pinch of salt	3 tablespoons water
3 tablespoons water	

Using the *Steel Blade,* process the flour, fat (shortening) and salt for a few seconds until the mixture resembles fine breadcrumbs.

With the motor still running, add the water down the feed tube and process for 15 to 20 seconds, until a dough is formed.

Wrap the dough in cling film (plastic wrap) and chill for 5 to 10 minutes before using. Use as required. Makes 500 g/1 lb pastry (basic pie dough).

Variation:
Use wholewheat flour instead of plain (all-purpose).

For a richer pastry for sweet and savoury flans (pies), use 250 g/8 oz (2 cups) plain (all-purpose) flour and 175 g/6 oz (¾ cup) chilled butter following the above method. Add one egg at the breadcrumb stage, then add just enough chilled water to form a ball.

For a sweet pastry, add 2 tablespoons sugar to the flour and proceed as above.

Choux Pastry (Paste)

Metric/Imperial	*American*
65 g/2½ oz butter	5 tablespoons butter
150 ml/¼ pint water	⅔ cup water
75 g/3 oz plain flour	¾ cup all-purpose flour
2 eggs	2 eggs

Place the butter and water in a saucepan over moderate heat and bring to the boil, stirring until the butter melts.

Remove from the heat and add the flour, stirring with a wooden spoon until the mixture binds together and leaves the sides of the pan cleanly.

Transfer the paste to the processor fitted with the *Steel Blade*. With the motor running, add the eggs down the feed tube, one at a time, and process until the dough is well mixed and smooth. Use as desired. Makes enough for about 12 éclairs.

Variations:

Sweet Choux Pastry (Paste): Add 25 g/1 oz (2 tablespoons) sugar to the butter and water in the saucepan.

Cheese Choux Pastry (Paste): Add 4 tablespoons (½ cup) grated cheese – Gruyère, Parmesan or mature (sharp) Cheddar – plus 1 teaspoon made mustard and a sprinkling of black or cayenne pepper to the prepared basic Choux Pastry.

Chocolate Éclairs: Using a piping bag fitted with a 1 cm/½ inch nozzle, pipe the mixture in 10 cm/4 inch lengths on a greased baking sheet. Bake in a preheated moderately hot oven (200°C/400°F, Gas Mark 6) for about 30 minutes. Remove, split lengthwise and cool. Fill with whipped cream and top with melted chocolate.

Profiteroles: Place heaped teaspoonfuls of the mixture well apart on a dampened baking sheet. Bake in a preheated moderately hot oven (200°C/400°F, Gas Mark 6) for 25-30 minutes. Slit down the side and cool. Fill with whipped cream. For chocolate sauce, melt 125 g/4 oz (4 squares) plain (semi-sweet) chocolate in a bowl over hot water. Stir in 2 tablespoons golden (light corn) syrup. Pour over the profiteroles while still hot. For a rich dessert, add a tablespoon of brandy or orange liqueur to the chocolate sauce.

Strawberry Puffs (McDougall's Flour)

Strawberry Puffs

Metric/Imperial	*American*
1 quantity Sweet Choux Pastry (see left)	1 quantity Sweet Choux Paste (see left)
300 ml/½ pint whipping cream	1¼ cups whipping cream
250 g/8 oz strawberries, hulled	½ lb strawberries, hulled
icing sugar for dusting	confectioners' sugar for dusting

Prepare the basic Sweet Choux Pastry (Paste) and spoon
into a piping (pastry) bag fitted with a 2 cm/¾ inch nozzle.
Run a greased baking sheet under cold water to dampen,
then pipe whirls of the choux mixture on to the baking
sheet. Bake in a preheated hot oven (220°C/425°F, Gas
Mark 7) for 30 minutes, until well risen and golden.
Remove from the baking tray and transfer to a wire rack.
Split each bun in half to allow the steam to escape.

   To make the filling, whip the cream until stiff enough to
hold its shape. Spoon in to a piping bag and pipe into the
base of each bun. Arrange the strawberries on top of the
cream and replace the tops of the puffs. Dust with icing
(confectioners') sugar to serve. Makes 10 to 15 puffs.

Soda Water Pastry

This light puff pastry is easier and cheaper to prepare than the conventional recipe that uses butter and the results are just as good.

Metric/Imperial
250 g/8 oz margarine, frozen
250 g/8 oz plain flour
pinch of salt
squeeze of lemon juice
175 ml/7 fl oz soda water, chilled

American
1 cup frozen margarine
2 cups all-purpose flour
pinch of salt
squeeze of lemon juice
¾ cup chilled soda water

Using the *Chip Plate,* process the frozen margarine to make margarine chips (French fries). Sift the flour and salt into a mixing bowl and stir in the margarine 'chips'. Add the squeeze of lemon and the chilled water. Using a palette knife (spatula), bring the mixture together to form a stiff dough.

Place the dough on a lightly floured surface and roll out to form a large rectangle. Fold the top third of the rectangle down and bring the bottom third up. Seal the edges of the parcel by striking firmly with the rolling pin. Give the dough a quarter of a turn so that the side edge is now closest to you and repeat the rolling and folding process. Cover and refrigerate for about 20 minutes.

Remove the dough and roll and fold the dough twice more. Return to the refrigerator for a further 20 minutes, then repeat the basic rolling and folding twice more so that the dough has been rolled six times in total. Allow the dough to rest in the refrigerator for a final 20 minutes before using it to top sweet or savoury pies. Makes 500 g/1 lb.

BREADS

A food processor really does take the hard work out of bread making because doughs are kneaded in less than a minute. Check your instruction manual for maximum quantities, and be careful not to overload the machine.

White Bread

Metric/Imperial	American
2 teaspoons active dried yeast	2 teaspoons active dried yeast
½ teaspoon sugar	½ teaspoon sugar
175 ml/7 fl oz warm water (hand hot)	¾ cup plus 2 tablespoons warm water (hand hot)
350 g/12 oz strong plain flour	3 cups bread flour
½ teaspoon salt	½ teaspoon salt
1 tablespoon oil	1 tablespoons oil

Sprinkle the yeast and sugar into the warm water and leave to stand for about 10 minutes, until the yeast is frothy.

Place the flour and salt in the processor fitted with the *Steel Blade* and process for a couple of seconds until sifted. With the motor running, add the oil and the yeast liquid in a steady stream down the feed tube. Continue processing until the mixture forms a dough, adding more water if necessary. Process for about 1 minute, until the dough is smooth and elastic. Transfer the dough to a greased bowl, cover with a damp cloth and leave in a warm place for about 1 to 1½ hours, until doubled in size.

Return the dough to the processor and, using the *Steel Blade,* process for about 10 seconds. Shape the dough into a small loaf or bread rolls and place on a greased baking sheet. Leave in a warm place for about 30 minutes, until doubled in size. Bake in a preheated hot oven (220°C/425°F, Gas Mark 7) for 25 to 30 minutes for a loaf, 10 to 15 minutes for bread rolls. The bread is cooked when it sounds hollow when tapped on the bottom. Makes one small loaf or 12 rolls.

Variations:

Wholewheat Bread: Use wholewheat flour in place of white. Sprinkle the shaped bread with seeds, coarse salt or whole grains before baking.

Herb Bread: Add 1 teaspoon dried or 1 tablespon chopped fresh herbs to the bread dough.

DON'T immerse the base or the motor of the machine in water.

Cheese Loaf

Metric/Imperial	American
250 g/8 oz wholemeal bread flour	2 cups wholewheat flour
1 teaspoon sea salt	1 teaspoon sea salt
1 teaspoon mustard powder	1 teaspoon mustard powder
125 g/4 oz Cheddar cheese, grated	1 cup grated Cheddar cheese
2 teaspoons active dried yeast	2 teaspoons active dried yeast
½ teaspoon sugar	½ teaspoon sugar
150 ml/¼ pint warm water (hand hot)	⅔ cup warm water (hand hot)

Put the flour, salt, mustard and cheese in the processor bowl and, using the *Steel Blade*, mix well. Stir the yeast and the sugar into the warm water. Set aside until frothy, then, with the motor running, pour the yeast mixture down the feed tube, adding just enough liquid to form the mixture into a dough.

Process the dough for about 1 minute, until smooth and elastic. Place the dough in a greased bowl. Cover with a damp cloth and leave in a warm place for about 1 hour, until doubled in size.

Return to the processor and process again for a few seconds, then fold into three and place in a greased, warmed 450 g/1 lb loaf tin (pan). Cover with a clean cloth and leave in a warm place for about 20 minutes, until the dough rises to the top of the tin (pan).

Bake in a preheated hot oven (220°C/425°F, Gas Mark 7) for 10 minutes, then reduce the heat to moderately hot (190°C/375°F, Gas Mark 5) and bake for a further 35 minutes. Turn out on to a wire rack and leave to cool completely. Makes one 450 g/1 lb loaf.

CAKES AND BISCUITS (COOKIES)

Small quantities of cake mixture can be prepared very quickly in a food processor. Turn off the processor and scrape down the sides of the bowl whenever necessary.

Standby Biscuits (Cookies)

Metric/Imperial	American
250 g/8 oz plain flour	2 cups all-purpose flour
1 teaspoon baking powder	1 teaspoon baking powder
125 g/4 oz butter, diced	½ cup butter, diced
175 g/6 oz caster sugar	¾ cup superfine sugar
1 teaspoon vanilla essence	1 teaspoon vanilla
1 egg	1 egg

Using the *Steel Blade,* process the flour and baking powder for a second to sift. Add the butter and process until the mixture resembles fine breadcrumbs. Add the sugar, vanilla and egg and process just until the mixture forms a ball. Turn out on to a lightly floured board.

Form the dough into a sausage about 5 cm/2 inches in diameter. Wrap in greaseproof (waxed) paper and chill until firm. Cut into 1 cm/½ inch thick slices and place on a greased baking sheet. Bake in a preheated moderately hot oven (190°C/375°F, Gas Mark 5) for 10 minutes or until golden. Leave on the tray for a minute or two then transfer to a wire rack to cool completely. Makes about 40.

Variations:
Add 50 g/2 oz (⅓ cup) of any of the following flavourings to the formed dough, using the on/off or pulse switch: coarsely grated chocolate, nuts, raisins, glacé (candied) cherries or mixed (candied) peel.

Standby Biscuits (Cookies)

Shortbread

Metric/Imperial	American
125 g/4 oz butter, chilled and diced	½ cup butter, chilled and diced
50 g/2 oz caster sugar	¼ cup superfine sugar
150 g/5 oz plain flour	1¼ cups all-purpose flour
pinch of salt	pinch of salt

Using the *Steel Blade,* process all the ingredients together until the mixture resembles fine breadcrumbs. Do not overprocess to the dough stage.

Press the mixture into an 18 cm/7 inch sandwich tin (layer cake pan). Mark eight portions with a knife and bake in a preheated moderate oven (180°C/350°F, Gas Mark 4) for 30 to 35 minutes, until golden brown and firm to the touch.

Cool in the tin and then transfer to a wire rack to cool completely. Makes 8 portions.

Victoria Sandwich

Metric/Imperial	American
175 g/6 oz butter or margarine, softened	¾ cup butter or margarine, softened
175 g/6 oz caster sugar	¾ cup superfine sugar
3 eggs	3 eggs
175 g/6 oz self-raising flour	1½ cups self-rising flour
1 teaspoon baking powder	1 teaspoon baking powder
To serve:	*To serve:*
jam	jam
icing sugar	confectioners' sugar

Grease two 18 cm/7 inch sandwich tins (layer cake pans) and line the bases with greaseproof (waxed) paper.

Using the *Steel Blade,* process the butter or margarine, sugar, eggs, flour and baking powder for about 20 seconds, until smooth.

Divide the mixture between the prepared tins (pans). Bake in a preheated moderate oven (160°C/325°F, Gas Mark 3) for 30 to 35 minutes, until the cakes are golden and springy to the touch. Turn out on to a wire rack to cool.

Sandwich the two layers together with jam and dredge the top with icing (confectioners') sugar. Makes one 18 cm/7 inch cake.

Variations:

Coffee: Add 1 tablespoon strong black coffee.

Chocolate: Add 2 tablespoons cocoa powder (unsweetened cocoa) in place of 2 tablespoons flour.

Scones

Metric/Imperial	*American*
250 g/8 oz self-raising flour	2 cups self-rising flour
1 teaspoon baking powder	1 teaspoon baking powder
pinch of salt	pinch of salt
50 g/2 oz caster sugar (for sweet scones only)	1/4 cup sugar (for sweet scones only)
50 g/2 oz butter, diced	1/4 cup butter, diced
about 150 ml/1/4 pint milk or soured milk	about 2/3 cup milk or soured milk

Using the *Steel Blade,* process the flour, baking powder and salt for a few seconds to sift. Add the sugar (if using) and butter and process until the mixture resembles fine breadcrumbs. Do not overprocess. With the motor running, add just enough milk down the feed tube to allow the mixture to form a ball. Again, do not overprocess. Transfer the dough to a floured board and roll out to 2.5 cm/1 inch thick. Cut into 5 cm/2 inch rounds and transfer to a floured baking sheet. Brush the tops with a little milk and bake in a preheated hot oven (220°C/425°F, Gas Mark 7) for 10 to 15 minutes. Makes 8 to 12.

Variations:

Cheese Scones: Add 75 g/3 oz (3/4 cup) grated cheese and 1/2 teaspoon mustard powder to the flour. Shape and bake as above.

Blue Cheese Ring: Add 50 g/2 oz (1/2 cup) crumbled blue cheese to the flour. Divide the dough into 8 equal pieces and form into balls. Place the balls in a 20 cm/8 inch round cake tin (pan) so they are just touching. Brush the tops with milk and bake in a moderately hot oven (200°C/400°F, Gas Mark 6) for about 25 minutes or until well risen and brown.

Avocado Ice Cream

Avocado Ice Cream

Metric/Imperial
2 large ripe avocados
75 g/3 oz full fat soft cheese
1 shallot, peeled
1 tablespoon lemon juice
2 tablespoons plain yogurt
1 teaspoon sugar
dash of Worcestershire
  sauce
pinch of ground nutmeg
pinch of paprika
salt
fresh black pepper
To Serve:
4 tablespoons mayonnaise
125 g/4 oz peeled prawns
parsley sprigs

American
2 large ripe avocados
6 tablespoons cream
  cheese
1 shallot, peeled
1 tablespoon lemon juice
2 tablespoons plain yogurt
1 teaspoon sugar
dash of Worcestershire
  sauce
pinch of ground nutmeg
pinch of paprika
salt
fresh black pepper
To Serve:
¼ cup mayonnaise
1 cup shelled, cooked
  shrimp
parsley sprigs

Peel the avocados and remove the stones. Using the *Steel Blade,* process the avocado and the remaining ingredients until well combined.

Pour into a freezer container and freeze for at least 1½ to 2 hours. Stir 2 or 3 times during the freezing process to prevent ice crystals forming. When the ice cream is frozen, cover and return to the freezer.

Soften the ice cream in the refrigerator for 1 hour before serving. Spoon into individual glasses and top each with a spoonful of mayonnaise and prawns (shrimp). Garnish each with parsley sprigs and serve at once. Serves 4.

Brandade

Metric/Imperial	*American*
350 g/12 oz white fish fillets, skinned	¾ lb white fish fillets, skinned
about 150 ml/¼ pint milk	about ⅔ cup milk
salt	salt
fresh black pepper	fresh black pepper
1 bay leaf	1 bay leaf
1 small onion, peeled	1 small onion, peeled
1 medium potato, boiled and peeled	1 medium potato, boiled and peeled
2 cloves garlic, peeled	2 cloves garlic, peeled
2 tablespoons olive oil	2 tablespoons olive oil
about 2 tablespoons lemon juice	about 2 tablespoons lemon juice
3-4 tablespoons double cream	3-4 tablespoons heavy cream

Place the fish in a saucepan with just enough milk to cover. Add salt, pepper and the bay leaf. Simmer gently for about 5 minutes, until the fish flakes easily. Drain.

Using the *Steel Blade,* process the onion, potato and garlic until mixed. (Do not overprocess or the potato will become sticky.) Add the fish and continue processing until smooth. With the motor running, add the olive oil, 1½ tablespoons lemon juice and 2 tablespoons of the cream. Taste and add more salt, pepper, lemon juice and cream if liked. Spoon into a serving dish, cover and chill until ready to serve. Serves 4.

Iced Camembert

Metric/Imperial	American
250 g/8 oz soft Camembert, cubed	½ lb soft Camembert, cubed
125 g/4 oz cottage cheese	½ cup curd cheese
250 ml/8 fl oz whipping cream	1 cup whipping cream
few drops of Tabasco sauce	few drops of hot pepper sauce
fresh black pepper	fresh black pepper
toast fingers to serve	toast fingers for serving
salt	salt

Place the Camembert in the processor fitted with the *Steel Blade*. Add the cottage (curd) cheese and process until smooth. With the motor running, add the cream, Tabasco (hot pepper sauce) and a little pepper and continue processing until the mixture is smooth. Adjust the seasoning to taste, transfer to a freezer container, cover and freeze until solid.

Remove the Iced Camembert from the freezer and soften in the refrigerator 1 hour before serving with toast fingers. Serves 4 to 6.

Liver Sausage Pâté

Metric/Imperial	American
350 g/12 oz liver sausage, cubed	¾ lb liverwurst, cubed
2 tablespoons single cream	2 tablespoons light cream
3 tablespoons mayonnaise	3 tablespoons mayonnaise
25 g/1 oz onion, chopped	¼ cup chopped onion
1½ teaspoons dried mixed herbs	1½ teaspoons Italian seasoning
salt	salt
fresh black pepper	fresh black pepper
1 tablespoon lemon juice	1 tablespoon lemon juice

Place all the ingredients in the processor and, using the *Steel Blade,* process until smooth. Adjust the seasoning, if necessary, transfer to a serving dish and chill until ready to serve. Serves 4.

Danish Blue Cheese Cake

Metric/Imperial	American
75 g/3 oz butter	6 tablespoons butter
175 g/6 oz wholemeal bran biscuits, crushed	1½ cups wholemeal bran biscuit crumbs
Topping:	Topping:
125 g/4 oz Danish blue cheese	¼ lb blue cheese
125 g/4 oz full fat soft cheese	½ cup cream cheese
1 clove garlic, peeled	1 clove garlic, peeled
2 large eggs, separated	2 large eggs, separated
1 teaspoon French mustard	1 teaspoon Dijon-style mustard
salt	salt
fresh black pepper	fresh black pepper
150 ml/¼ pint double cream	⅔ cup heavy cream
3 teaspoons gelatine	3 teaspoons gelatin
4 tablespoons hot water	4 tablespoons hot water
To garnish:	To garnish:
cucumber slices	cucumber slices
black grapes	black grapes

Melt the butter in a small saucepan over moderate heat and stir in the biscuit crumbs. Mix well, then press firmly into the base of a greased 20 cm/8 inch loose-bottomed (springform) cake tin (pan). Refrigerate until ready to use.

To make the topping, place the blue and cream cheeses and the garlic in the processor and, using the *Steel Blade*, process until creamy. Add the egg yolks, mustard, salt, pepper and cream and blend until smooth. Sprinkle the gelatine over the hot water and stir until dissolved. Add to the cheese mixture down the feed tube, mix well and set the mixture aside until just on the point of setting. Whisk the egg whites until stiff, add to the bowl and, using the on/off or pulse switch, fold them in until just blended. Pour the mixture on to the biscuit base and smooth the surface.

Refrigerate for 3 to 4 hours, until set. Serve the Danish Blue cheese cake garnished with the cucumber slices and black grapes. Serves 6-8.

Duck and Orange Terrine

Duck and Orange Terrine

Metric/Imperial	*American*
1 large duck portion or 250 g/8 oz duck flesh, including some skin	1 large duck portion or ½ lb duck flesh, including some skin
125 g/4 oz lean bacon rashers, rind removed	¼ lb bacon slices
1 onion, peeled	1 onion, peeled
1 clove garlic, peeled	1 clove garlic, peeled
grated rind of ½ orange	grated rind of ½ orange
2 tablespoons orange juice	2 tablespoons orange juice
1 tablespoon brandy	1 tablespoon brandy
1 egg	1 egg
salt	salt
fresh black pepper	fresh black pepper
To garnish:	*To garnish:*
orange slices	orange slices
fresh bay leaves	fresh bay leaves
a little liquid aspic jelly	a little liquid aspic jelly

Strip the flesh off the duck portion, if using. Using the *Steel Blade,* process the duck with the bacon, onion and garlic clove until well minced (ground). Add the orange rind and juice, brandy, egg, salt and pepper and mix thoroughly.

Grease a 600 ml/1 pint (2½ cup) ovenproof terrine and spoon in the mixture, pressing down well. Cover and stand in a roasting pan containing about 4 cm/1½ inches hot water. Cook in a preheated moderate oven (180°C/350°F, Gas Mark 4) for 30 minutes. Uncover and cook for a further 35 to 40 minutes or until cooked through. Remove from the water bath and leave until cold.

Arrange the orange slices and bay leaves on top and pour over a layer of aspic jelly which is on the point of setting. Chill until the garnish is set. Turn the terrine out on to a serving plate. Serve, sliced, with crusty bread or hot toast and butter. Serves 4.

Potted Ham en Cocotte

Metric/Imperial	*American*
1 × 100 g/3½ oz pack honey roast ham, chilled	1 × ¼ lb pack honey roast ham, chilled
2 spring onions	2 scallions
2 tablespoons grated Parmesan cheese	2 tablespoons grated Parmesan cheese
3 eggs, separated	3 eggs, separated
1 tablespoon dry white wine	1 tablespoon dry white wine
2-3 drops of Tabasco sauce	2-3 drops of hot pepper sauce

Place the ham and spring onions (scallions) in the processor and using the *Steel Blade,* process until finely chopped. Add the cheese, egg yolks, wine and Tabasco (hot pepper sauce) and mix. Whisk the egg whites until soft peaks form. Fold into the ham mixture, using the on/off or pulse switch.

Divide the mixture between four greased individual ovenproof dishes and bake in a preheated moderately hot oven (200°C/400°F, Gas Mark 6) for 18 to 20 minutes or until puffed and golden. Serve potted ham with crusty rolls and salad as a lunch or supper dish. Serves 4.
Illustrated on pages 2 and 3.

Cheese Soup

Metric/Imperial	American
1 large onion, peeled	1 large onion, peeled
25 g/1 oz butter	2 tablespoons butter
25 g/1 oz plain flour	¼ cup all-purpose flour
1 teaspoon mustard powder	1 teaspoon dry ground mustard
salt	salt
fresh black pepper	fresh black pepper
600 ml/1 pint milk	2½ cups milk
150 ml/¼ pint chicken stock	⅔ cup chicken stock
125 g/4 oz Cheddar cheese, chilled and cubed	¼ lb Cheddar Cheese, chilled and cubed

Using the *Steel Blade,* chop the onion. Melt the butter in a large saucepan over moderate heat, add the onion and sauté until soft. Stir in the flour, mustard and salt and pepper to taste. Gradually add the milk and stock, stirring until the soup boils and thickens slightly.

Reduce the heat, cover and simmer for 15 minutes, stirring occasionally.

Using the *Shredding Plate,* shred the cheese, then add to the soup and stir until melted. Do not boil the soup once the cheese has been added.

Serve in individual warmed bowls. Serves 4.

Curried Cauliflower Soup

Metric/Imperial	American
1 small onion, peeled	1 small onion, peeled
50 g/2 oz butter or margarine	¼ cup butter or margarine
2 teaspoons curry powder	2 teaspoons curry powder
250 g/8 oz cauliflower florets, roughly chopped	½ lb cauliflower florets, roughly chopped
600 ml/1 pint milk	2½ cups milk
salt	salt
2 tablespoons single cream to serve	2 tablespoons light cream for serving

Using the *Steel Blade,* chop the onion. Melt the butter or margarine in a large saucepan over moderate heat, add the onion and curry powder and sauté gently until soft. Add the cauliflower and sauté for a further 5 minutes, stirring frequently. Stir in 450 ml/¾ pint (2 cups) of the milk and add salt to taste. Bring to the boil, half cover and simmer for 15 to 20 minutes, stirring occasionally, until the cauliflower is soft.

Remove from the heat and leave to cool a little. Using the *Steel Blade,* process the mixture until smooth.

Return the soup to a clean pan, stir in the remaining milk and reheat until bubbling. Adjust the seasoning if necessary. Add more milk if a thinner consistency is preferred.

Serve hot in individual warmed soup bowls with a swirl of cream on top. Serves 4.

Tomato and Mozzarella Salad with Basil

Metric/Imperial	American
500 g/1 lb small tomatoes, peeled	1 lb small tomatoes, peeled
250 g/8 oz mozzarella cheese, partially frozen	½ lb mozzarella cheese, partially frozen
salt	salt
fresh black pepper	fresh black pepper
3 tablespoons olive oil	3 tablespoons olive oil
1 tablespoon white wine vinegar	1 tablespoon white wine vinegar
1½ tablespoons chopped basil	1½ tablespoons chopped basil

Using the *Slicing Plate,* slice the tomatoes thinly, then arrange on one half of a flat serving dish. Slice the cheese and arrange the slices on the other half of the dish.

Season the tomatoes with salt and pepper and the cheese with pepper only. Pour over the oil and vinegar and scatter the chopped basil over all. Allow to stand for at least 15 minutes before serving. Serves 4.

DO use the food pusher when feeding ingredients on to the shredding or slicing plates; *never* use any other implement or your fingers.

Braised Red Cabbage

Metric/Imperial	American
500 g/1 lb red cabbage	1 lb red cabbage
1 large onion, peeled	1 large onion, peeled
1 cooking apple, peeled and cored	1 tart apple, pared and cored
4 tablespoons sultanas	⅓ cup golden raisins
150 ml/¼ pint water, stock or dry red wine	⅔ cup water, stock or dry red wine
3 tablespoons wine vinegar	3 tablespoons wine vinegar
salt	salt
fresh black pepper	fresh black pepper
1 tablespoon sugar (optional)	1 tablespoon sugar (optional)

Using the *Slicing Plate,* finely slice the cabbage, onion and apple in individual batches, then place in a saucepan with the remaining ingredients. Bring to the boil, cover, reduce the heat and simmer gently for 30 to 40 minutes or until the cabbage is tender. If there is any liquid in the base of the pan, uncover and cook until the liquid has evaporated. Serve hot or chilled with roast or grilled (broiled) meats or fish. Serves 4.

Braised Red Cabbage

Potatoes Layered with Herbs

Metric/Imperial	American
2 onions, peeled	2 onions, peeled
750 g/1½ lb potatoes, peeled	1½ lb potatoes, peeled
2 teaspoons dried basil or rosemary	2 teaspoons dried basil or rosemary
fresh black pepper	fresh black pepper
500 ml/17 fl oz chicken stock	2 cups chicken stock
25 g/1 oz butter	2 tablespoons butter

Using the *Slicing Plate,* slice the onions and the potatoes in individual batches. Layer them in a well greased ovenproof dish, sprinkling each layer with a generous amount of herbs and black pepper.

Pour over the chicken stock, dot with butter and sprinkle with a little more basil or rosemary. Bake in a preheated moderate oven (180°C/350°F, Gas Mark 4) until the potatoes are tender and the top is golden. Serves 4.

Nutty Carrot Salad

Metric/Imperial	American
500 g/1 lb carrots, peeled	1 lb carrots, peeled
75 g/3 oz raisins	½ cup raisins
25 g/1 oz hazelnuts, chopped	¼ cup roughly chopped hazelnuts
grated rind and juice of 1 orange	grated rind and juice of 1 orange
4 tablespoons soured cream	¼ cup sour cream
salt	salt
fresh black pepper	fresh black pepper
chopped fresh parsley to garnish	chopped fresh parsley for garnish

Using the *Shredding Plate,* grate the carrots, then place in a bowl with the raisins, chopped nuts, orange rind and juice, soured cream, salt and pepper. Toss thoroughly and serve sprinkled with chopped parsley. Serves 6.

Raisin and Yogurt Coleslaw

Metric/Imperial	American
500 g/1 lb white cabbage	1 lb white cabbage
½ bunch radishes	½ bunch radishes
4 spring onions	4 scallions
75 g/3 oz raisins	½ cup raisins
50 g/2 oz dried apricots	⅓ cup dried apricots
1 green pepper, cored and seeded	1 green pepper, seeded
Yogurt Dressing:	Yogurt Dressing:
150 ml/¼ pint plain yogurt	⅔ cup plain yogurt
2 teaspoons French mustard	2 teaspoons Dijon-style mustard
1 clove garlic, peeled	1 clove garlic, peeled
1 tablespoon clear honey	1 tablespoon clear honey
salt	salt
fresh black pepper	fresh black pepper
½ teaspoon dried basil	½ teaspoon dried basil

Using the *Slicing Plate,* shred the cabbage, the radishes and spring onions (scallions). Place these vegetables in a salad bowl with the raisins. Replace the slicing plate with the *Steel Blade* and finely chop the apricots and green pepper, then add to the salad bowl.

Place all the dressing ingredients in the processor bowl and, using the *Plastic or Nylon Blade,* process until smooth. Pour over the salad and toss well. Chill for 20 to 30 minutes before serving. Serves 6-8.

Turnip and Watercress Purée

Metric/Imperial	American
500 g/1 lb turnips, peeled	1 lb turnips, peeled
250 g/8 oz potatoes, peeled	½ lb potatoes, peeled
1 bunch watercress	1 bunch watercress
salt	salt
fresh black pepper	fresh black pepper

Using the *Chip Plate,* cut the turnips and potatoes into chips (French fries). Place in a saucepan with just enough water to cover and bring to the boil. Cover, reduce the heat and simmer for about 20 minutes or until tender.

Remove the coarse stalks from the watercress, reserving several sprigs for garnish. Add the watercress leaves to the pan and continue cooking for 1 minute. Drain, reserving the cooking liquid.

Transfer the vegetables to the bowl of the processor fitted with the *Steel Blade* and process until smooth, adding a little of the cooking liquid if necessary. Adjust the seasoning and reheat, if liked. Turn into a warm serving dish and top with the reserved watercress sprigs. Serve with roast game or poultry. Serves 4.

Potato Roulade

Metric/Imperial	*American*
1 kg/2 lb potatoes, peeled	2 lb potatoes, peeled
1 onion, peeled	1 onion, peeled
2 parsley sprigs	2 parsley sprigs
salt	salt
fresh black pepper	fresh black pepper
oil for deep-frying	oil for deep frying
Filling:	*Filling:*
125 g/4 oz frozen spinach	¼ lb frozen spinach
75 g/3 oz full fat soft cheese	⅓ cup cream cheese
2 teaspoons mild curry paste	2 teaspoons mild curry paste
1 teaspoon lemon juice	1 teaspoon lemon juice

Cook the potatoes in boiling salted water until tender. Meanwhile, using the *Steel Blade,* chop the onion and parsley. Drain the potatoes and allow to cool a little. Roughly chop, then add to the processor bowl with the onion and parsley mixture, salt and pepper and process for about 3 minutes, until very sticky and elastic. Roll out to form an oblong measuring about 15×20 cm/6×8 inches.

Place all the ingredients for the filling in the processor fitted with the *Steel Blade* and mix thoroughly. Spread over the potato dough and roll up, Swiss (jelly) roll style. Refrigerate until well chilled, then cut into 10 to 12 slices.

Heat the oil until a cube of bread browns in 30 seconds (190°C/375°F). Sauté the roulade slices in the hot oil until golden. Drain and serve with a salad. Serves 6.

Avocado Stuffed Tomatoes

Avocado Stuffed Tomatoes

Metric/Imperial	*American*
4 large tomatoes	4 large tomatoes
salt	salt
1 large ripe avocado	1 large ripe avocado
grated rind and juice of ½ lemon	grated rind and juice of ½ lemon
125 g/4 oz full fat soft cheese	½ cup cream cheese
1 clove garlic, peeled	1 clove garlic, peeled
1 small onion, peeled	1 small onion, peeled
few drops of Tabasco sauce	few drops of hot pepper sauce
fresh black pepper	fresh black pepper

Cut the tops off the tomatoes and remove seeds. Sprinkle with salt and turn the tomatoes upside down to drain.

Halve the avocado and remove the stone. Scoop out the flesh and using the *Steel Blade*, process the avocado with all the remaining ingredients until the mixture is smooth. Spoon the mixture into the tomatoes and replace the tomato lids. Chill until ready to serve. Serves 4.

Variation:

For special occasions, top the tomatoes with a little lumpfish roe instead of the lids and serve as a starter.

Fennel, Prawn and Sesame Salad

Metric/Imperial	*American*
1 large bulb fennel	1 large bulb fennel
250 g/8 oz courgettes	½ lb zucchini
250 g/8 oz French beans, trimmed	½ lb green beans, trimmed
1 small lettuce, leaves separated and washed	1 small head lettuce, leaves separated and washed
125 g/4 oz cooked prawns	1 cup cooked shrimp
2 tablespoons sesame seeds, toasted	2 tablespoons sesame seeds, toasted
Dressing:	*Dressing:*
150 ml/¼ pint soured cream	⅔ cup sour cream
1 teaspoon made mustard	1 teaspoon made mustard
grated rind of 1 lemon	grated rind of 1 lemon
salt	salt
fresh black pepper	fresh black pepper

Using the *Slicing Plate,* finely slice the fennel and courgettes (zucchini). Bring a pan of water to the boil and blanch the courgette slices and French beans for 1 minute. Drain and place under cold running water until cold. Drain again and pat dry.

Arrange the lettuce leaves in a serving bowl and top with the fennel, courgettes, beans and prawns (shrimp).

For the dressing, place the sour cream, mustard and lemon rind in the food processor fitted with the *Steel Blade* and process until well blended. Adjust the seasoning. Pour over the salad and sprinkle with sesame seeds. Serves 4.

Ratatouille

Metric/Imperial	American
2 Spanish onions, peeled	2 Spanish onions, peeled
4 tablespoons oil	¼ cup oil
2 medium aubergines	2 medium size eggplant
2 cloves garlic, peeled	2 cloves garlic, peeled
350 g/12 oz courgettes	¾ lb zucchini
1 red pepper, cored and seeded	1 red pepper, seeded
1 green pepper, cored and seeded	1 green pepper, seeded
750 g/1½ lb tomatoes, skinned and seeded	1½ lb tomatoes, peeled and seeded
3 tablespoons tomato purée	3 tablespoons tomato paste
salt	salt
fresh black pepper	fresh black pepper
1 bay leaf	1 bay leaf
sprig of thyme	sprig of thyme
2 tablespoons chopped fresh parsley to serve	2 tablespoons chopped fresh parsley for serving

Using the *Slicing Plate,* slice the Spanish onions. Heat the oil in a large heavy-based saucepan and gently sauté the onions until soft and lightly coloured.

Using the *Steel Blade,* roughly chop the aubergines (egg plant) and garlic, then add to the saucepan and cook for 3 to 4 minutes, stirring.

Using the *Slicing Blade,* slice the courgettes (zucchini) and red and green peppers in individual batches. Add to the saucepan and continue cooking for 4 to 5 minutes. Slice the tomatoes and add to the other vegetables.

Stir in the remaining ingredients, cover and cook over a gentle heat for 20 to 30 minutes, tossing occasionally to ensure even cooking. When cooked, the vegetables should be tender, but still firm. Remove the bay leaf.

Stir in the parsley and serve hot. Serves 4 to 6.

Helpful Hint
Save washing up time by chopping a recipe's dry ingredients before chopping the wet ones.

Pasta Salad

Metric/Imperial	American
250 g/8 oz wholewheat pasta shapes	1⅔ cup wholewheat pasta shapes
1 onion, peeled	1 onion, peeled
1 small green pepper, cored and seeded	1 small green pepper, seeded
1 small aubergine	1 small eggplant
2 tablespoons oil	2 tablespoons oil
2 tomatoes, skinned and chopped	2 tomatoes, peeled and chopped
salt	salt
fresh black pepper	fresh black pepper
Dressing:	*Dressing:*
150 ml/¼ pint vegetable oil	⅔ cup vegetable oil
4 tablespoons dry white wine, vinegar or lemon juice	¼ cup dry white wine, vinegar or lemon juice
1 teaspoon made mustard	1 teaspoon prepared mustard
pinch of sugar	pinch of sugar
½ teaspoon each dried marjoram and oregano	½ teaspoon each dried marjoram and oregano
1 clove garlic, peeled	1 clove garlic, peeled

Cook the pasta in boiling salted water for about 15 minutes, until just tender. Drain.

Using the *Slicing Plate,* finely slice the onions, pepper and aubergine (eggplant) in individual batches.

Heat the oil in a frying pan (skillet) and lightly sauté the vegetables until just tender. Add the tomatoes, pasta, salt and pepper and mix well. Remove from the heat and transfer the vegetables and pasta to a salad bowl.

For the dressing, place all the ingredients in the processor fitted with the *Steel Blade* and process until well mixed. Pour over the vegetables, toss well and set aside to cool. Serve at room temperature. Serves 4.

Helpful Hint
If a recipe requires you to mix together ingredients of different textures it is best to chop the hard ingredients before chopping the soft ones.

Irish Hotpot

Metric/Imperial	American
4 chicken joints	4 chicken pieces
2 tablespoons flour seasoned with salt and fresh black pepper	2 tablespoons flour seasoned with salt and fresh black pepper
40 g/1½ oz butter	3 tablespoons butter
1 tablespoon oil	1 tablespoon oil
1 tablespoon chopped fresh thyme	1 tablespoon chopped fresh thyme
salt	salt
fresh black pepper	fresh black pepper
2 large carrots, peeled	2 large carrots, peeled
3 celery sticks	3 celery sticks
250 g/8 oz white cabbage	½ lb white cabbage
300 ml/½ pint chicken stock	1¼ cups chicken stock
150 ml/¼ pint stout	⅔ cup dark beer
2 teaspoons dark brown sugar	2 teaspoons dark brown sugar
4 medium potatoes, peeled	4 medium-size potatoes, peeled
1 tablespoon melted butter	1 tablespoon melted butter

Dust the chicken joints in seasoned flour. Melt the butter and oil in a large frying pan (skillet) and sauté the chicken until golden on all sides. Stir in most of the thyme and salt and pepper to taste.

Using the *Slicing Plate,* thickly slice the carrots and celery and shred the cabbage. Transfer half the vegetables to the base of a deep casserole. Arrange the chicken on top, followed by the remaining sliced vegetables. In a small saucepan, heat the stock, stout (dark beer) and brown sugar gently and stir until the sugar dissolves. Pour into the casserole.

Using the *Slicing Plate,* finely slice the potatoes, then carefully arrange on top of the vegetables. Brush with the melted butter and sprinkle with the remaining thyme.

Cover and cook in a moderate oven (180°C/350°F, Gas Mark 4) for 1 hour. Remove the cover and continue cooking for a further 35 to 40 minutes or until golden. Serves 4.

Irish Hotpot
(British Chicken Information Service)

Derby Bacon and Apple Bake

Metric/Imperial	American
15 g/½ oz butter	1 tablespoon butter
625 g/1¼ lb potatoes, peeled	1¼ lb potatoes, peeled
salt	salt
fresh black pepper	fresh black pepper
2 tablespoons chopped fresh sage	2 tablespoons chopped fresh sage
500 g/1 lb tomatoes, skinned	1 lb tomatoes, peeled
250 g/8 oz onions, peeled	½ lb onions, peeled
350 g/12 oz apples	¾ lb apples
250 g/8 oz lean bacon rashers, rinds removed	½ lb lean bacon slices

Butter a shallow casserole or pie dish. Using the *Slicing Plate,* slice the potatoes, and place in the base of the dish. Sprinkle with salt, pepper and some of the sage. Slice the tomatoes, lay on top of the potatoes and season in the same way. Repeat with the onions and apples. Top with the bacon rashers (slices).

Cover and bake in a preheated moderate oven (180°C/350°F, Gas Mark 4) for 40 minutes. Uncover and cook for a further 10 minutes or until the bacon is golden and vegetables are tender. Serve with a green salad. Serves 4.

Chicken and Ham Croquettes

Metric/Imperial	American
25 g/1 oz butter	2 tablespoons butter
25 g/1 oz plain flour	¼ cup all-purpose flour
150 ml/¼ pint milk	⅔ cup milk
salt	salt
fresh black pepper	fresh black pepper
125 g/4 oz cooked chicken, boned	¼ lb cooked chicken, boned
125 g/4 oz cooked ham, diced	¼ lb cooked ham, diced
50 g/2 oz mushrooms	½ cup mushrooms
grated rind and juice of 1 lemon	grated rind and juice of 1 lemon
2 parsley sprigs	2 parsley sprigs
For deep-frying:	For deep-frying:
1 tablespoon plain flour	1 tablespoon all-purpose flour
1 egg, lightly beaten	1 egg, lightly beaten
50 g/2 oz dried breadcrumbs	½ cup dried bread crumbs
vegetable oil	vegetable oil

Melt the butter in a saucepan over moderate heat. Add the flour and cook for a few minutes, stirring constantly. Remove from the heat and gradually stir in the milk. Return to the heat and bring to the boil, stirring constantly. Remove from the heat and season with salt and pepper.

Place the remaining ingredients in the food processor bowl fitted with the *Steel Blade* and process until finely chopped and well mixed. Add the meat mixture to the sauce and mix well. Set aside until cold.

Divide the mixture into 4 equal parts and form into rounds. Coat the rounds with flour, then the beaten egg and breadcrumbs. Refrigerate for at least 30 minutes until well chilled.

Heat the oil in a deep-fat fryer to 190°C/375°F or until a cube of stale bread turns golden brown in 30 seconds. Deep-fry the croquettes for about 10 minutes until golden brown, turning occasionally to ensure an even colour. Serve Chicken and Ham Croquettes hot with a mixed salad and French bread. Serves 4.

Chicken Gougère

Metric/Imperial	*American*
1 quantity Savoury Choux pastry, see page 26	1 quantity Savoury Choux Paste, see page 26
Filling:	*Filling:*
1 onion, peeled	1 onion, peeled
25 g/1 oz butter	2 tablespoons butter
15 g/½ oz plain flour	1 tablespoon all-purpose flour
300 ml/½ pint chicken stock	1¼ cups chicken stock
125 g/4 oz button mushrooms	1 cup button mushrooms
500 g/1 lb cooked chicken	1 lb cooked chicken
3 tomatoes, skinned, seeded and quartered	3 tomatoes, peeled, seeded and quartered
pinch of dried tarragon	pinch of dried tarragon
1 tablespoon chopped fresh parsley	1 tablespoon chopped fresh parsley
salt	salt
fresh black pepper	fresh black pepper
1 tablespoon grated Parmesan cheese	1 tablespoon grated Parmesan cheese

Grease a 1.2 litre/2 pint (5 cup) gratin dish and spoon the choux pastry around the edge to form a border. Set aside.

Using the *Steel Blade,* chop the onion. Melt the butter in a saucepan, add the onion; sauté gently for 5 minutes, until soft and transparent. Stir in the flour and cook for 2 to 3 minutes. Remove from the heat and add the stock.

Using the *Slicing Blade,* slice the mushrooms, then add to the saucepan and bring to the boil.

Using the *Steel Blade,* cut the chicken into even pieces.

Allow the sauce to cool, then fold in the chicken, tomatoes, herbs, and add salt and pepper to taste.

Spoon the mixture into the centre of the choux pastry ring, and sprinkle with the Parmesan cheese.

Bake in a preheated moderately hot oven (200°C/400°F, Gas Mark 6) for 45 minutes, until the pastry is risen and golden. Reduce the heat to moderate (180°C/350°F, Gas Mark 4) and continue cooking for 15-20 minutes to set the pastry. Serves 4.

Hot Cheese Rolls (The Danish Dairy Board)

Hot Cheese Rolls

Metric/Imperial	*American*
4-5 crusty bread rolls	4-5 crusty bread rolls
250 g/8 oz Danish Samsoe cheese, cubed	½ lb Danish Samsoe cheese, cubed
2 eggs	2 eggs
½ teaspoon made mustard	½ teaspoon prepared mustard
butter for spreading	butter for spreading
watercress sprigs to garnish	watercress sprigs for garnish

Cut the top off each roll and scoop out the soft centre, leaving a shell. Place the tops, loose bread and cheese in the processor fitted with the *Steel Blade*; process until the crumbs are mixed with the cheese. Do not overprocess. Add eggs, mustard, salt and pepper; process until mixed.

Spread the inside of the rolls with butter, then fill with the cheese mixture. Place on a baking sheet and bake in a preheated moderately hot oven (200°C/400°F, Gas Mark 6) for 15 minutes. Garnish with watercress and serve with a crisp cabbage and apple salad. Serves 4.

Stir-Fried Liver with Vegetables

Metric/Imperial	American
25 g/1 oz cornflour	2 tablespoons cornstarch
3 tablespoons soy sauce	3 tablespoons soy sauce
2 tablespoons dry sherry	2 tablespoons dry sherry
2 celery sticks	2 stalks celery
125 g/4 oz white cabbage	¼ lb white cabbage
250 g/8 oz calves' liver, partially frozen	½ lb calves' liver, partially frozen
50 g/2 oz mushrooms	½ cup mushrooms
3 tablespoons oil	3 tablespoons oil
1 clove garlic, peeled	1 clove garlic, peeled
1 onion, peeled	1 onion, peeled
1 × 2.5 cm/1 inch piece fresh root ginger, peeled	1 × 1 inch piece fresh root ginger, peeled
2 carrots	2 carrots
75 g/3 oz bean sprouts	1½ cups bean sprouts
1 tablespoon clear honey	1 tablespoon clear honey
1 tablespoon brown sugar	1 tablespoon brown sugar
1 tablespoon wine vinegar	1 tablespoon wine vinegar
salt	salt
fresh black pepper	fresh black pepper

Mix 1 tablespoon of the cornflour (cornstarch) to a paste with 1 tablespoon each soy sauce and sherry in a bowl.

Using the *Slicing Plate,* slice the celery and cabbage. Set aside. Finely slice the liver and the mushrooms, then stir into the cornflour mixture and set aside.

Heat half the oil in a wok or large frying pan (skillet). Using the *Steel Blade,* chop the garlic, onion and ginger, then add to the oil. Sauté for about 3 minutes, until soft.

Fit the processor with the *Shredding Plate,* and grate the carrots. Add to the onion mixture with the reserved celery, cabbage, and bean sprouts. Cook for 5 minutes, stirring frequently. Mix together the remaining ingredients. Add to the vegetables and cook for a further 3 to 4 minutes.

Meanwhile, heat the remaining oil in a separate wok or frying pan, add the liver and mushroom mixture and stir-fry over a brisk heat for 5 minutes until the liver juices turn pink. Transfer the vegetables to a warm serving dish, then spoon the liver on top. Serve with boiled rice. Serves 4.

Parsley Meatballs with Cheese

Metric/Imperial	American
2 thick slices white bread, cubed	2 thick slices white bread, cubed
3 parsley sprigs	3 parsley sprigs
85 ml/3 fl oz dry white wine	6 tablespoons dry white wine
500 g/1 lb lean beef, cubed	1 lb lean beef, cubed
50 g/2 oz grated Parmesan cheese	½ cup grated Parmesan cheese
salt	salt
fresh black pepper	fresh black pepper
2 egg yolks	2 egg yolks
125 g/4 oz mozzarella or Cheddar cheese, cubed	1 cup cubed mozzarella or Cheddar cheese
oil for sautéing	oil for sautéing
noodles, to serve	noodles, to serve

Using the *Steel Blade,* process the bread and parsley until
fine crumbs are formed and the mixture is well mixed. Add
to the wine in a bowl and leave to soak for 15 minutes.
Place half the meat in the processor and, using the on/off
or pulse switch, process until minced (ground). Remove
and repeat with the remaining meat. Combine the meat,
grated Parmesan cheese, salt, pepper and egg yolks with
the crumb mixture until well mixed. Divide into about 16
even-sized pieces, and mould each one around a piece of
mozzarella or Cheddar cheese so that the cheese is
completely enclosed.

Heat the oil in a frying pan (skillet) and sauté the meat-
balls for about 6 minutes, turning to brown evenly. Serve
on a bed of noodles. Serves 4.

DON'T overload the processor. Read all the instructions
provided and check with the manufacturer's manual, the
dry and liquid capacities of your machine. If you add too
much liquid you will not only flood the kitchen but some of
the liquid could seep into the motor, causing permanent
damage.

If, however, you overwork the machine an automatic cut
out should activate before you blow out the motor.

Brazil Nut Loaf

Metric/Imperial
250 g/8 oz Brazil nuts,
  shelled
2 large slices wholemeal
  bread with crusts, cubed
1 tablespoon oil
4 streaky bacon rashers,
  rinds removed
2 onions, peeled
1 clove garlic, peeled
1 parsley sprig
1 thyme sprig
salt
fresh black pepper
1 egg
1 teaspoon Worcestershire
  sauce

American
½ lb Brazil nuts, shelled
2 large slices wholewheat
  bread with crusts, cubed
1 tablespoon oil
4 bacon slices
2 onions, peeled
1 clove garlic, peeled
1 parsley sprig
1 thyme sprig
salt
fresh black pepper
1 egg
1 teaspoon Worcestershire
  sauce

Place the nuts and bread in the processor fitted with the *Steel Blade* and process until just coarsely ground. Remove and reserve. Finely chop the bacon, onions, garlic, parsley and thyme.

Heat the oil in a large frying pan (skillet) over moderate heat and gently sauté the bacon, onions, garlic, parsley and thyme for 4 to 5 minutes, until soft. Remove the pan from the heat, add the ground nuts and bread, salt and pepper and mix well. Lightly beat the egg with the Worcestershire sauce, then add to the nut mixture and mix together thoroughly to bind.

Press the mixture into a lightly greased 500 g/1 lb (4 cup) loaf tin (pan) and level the surface. Bake in a preheated moderately hot oven (190°C/375°F, Gas Mark 5) for 40 minutes, until the top is crisp and lightly browned.

Turn the loaf out on to a serving dish and serve hot. Alternatively, leave to cool in the tin, then turn out and serve cold with sliced tomatoes. Serves 4 to 6.

Helpful Hint
To make your own potato crisps (chips), thinly slice raw potatoes, then fry in deep hot fat until golden.

Dinner Party Dishes

Tuna Mould

Metric/Imperial	American
1 tablespoon gelatine	1 tablespoon gelatin
2 tablespoons water	2 tablespoons water
25 g/1 oz butter	2 tablespoons butter
25 g/1 oz plain flour	¼ cup all-purpose flour
300 ml/½ pint milk	1¼ cups milk
salt	salt
fresh black pepper	fresh black pepper
1 × 200 g/7 oz can tuna in oil	1 × 7 oz can tuna in oil
150 ml/¼ pint soured cream	⅔ cup sour cream
1 tablespoon tomato purée	1 tablespoon tomato paste
2 teaspoons anchovy essence	2 teaspoons anchovy essence
grated rind and juice of ½ lemon	grated rind and juice of ½ lemon
1 egg, separated	1 egg, separated
To garnish:	For garnish:
cucumber slices	cucumber slices
125 g/4 oz prawns	⅔ cup shrimp

Soak the gelatine in the water until soft. Melt the butter in a saucepan over moderate heat, stir in the flour and cook for a few minutes, stirring constantly, to form a roux. Remove from the heat, add the milk, salt and pepper, then return to the heat and bring to the boil. Simmer for 2 minutes, stirring, remove from the heat again and add the gelatine. Stir until dissolved.

Place the tuna and the oil from the can in the food processor fitted with the *Steel Blade*. Add the soured cream, tomato purée (paste), anchovy essence, lemon rind and juice, the egg yolk, gelatine mixture, salt and pepper. Process until well mixed. Whisk the egg white until stiff, then add to the processor bowl and, using the on/off or pulse switch, process until the egg white is just folded in.

Turn into a 900 ml/1½ pint (4½ cup) fish mould and refrigerate until set. Invert on to a serving dish and serve garnished with cucumber slices and prawns (shrimp). Serves 4.

Tuna Mould

Hollandaise Sauce

A savoury butter sauce to serve with grilled (broiled) meat and fish.

Metric/Imperial
3 egg yolks
2 tablespoons lemon juice
½ teaspoon prepared
   mustard
250 g/8 oz butter
fresh black pepper

American
3 egg yolks
2 tablespoons lemon juice
½ teaspoon made mustard
1 cup butter
fresh black pepper

Using the *Steel Blade,* combine the egg yolks, lemon juice and mustard. Heat the butter in a small saucepan over low heat to the point where it is just beginning to bubble. With the motor running, pour the hot butter down the feed tube and continue processing for about 1 minute, until the sauce is thick and creamy. Taste the sauce and add black pepper and a little more lemon juice, if necessary. Makes 300 ml/½ pint (1¼ cups).
Variations:
Béarnaise Sauce: Add 1 spring onion (scallion) when processing the egg yolks, and use 1 tablespoon tarragon vinegar and ½ teaspoon dried tarragon in place of the lemon juice.
Mousseline Sauce: Fold 4 tablespoons lightly whipped cream into the Hollandaise Sauce just before serving.

Chicken with Tuna Sauce

Metric/Imperial	American
4 chicken breasts, boned and skinned	4 chicken breasts, boned and skinned
1 onion, peeled and sliced	1 onion, peeled and sliced
1 bay leaf	1 bay leaf
strip of lemon rind	strip of lemon rind
salt	salt
fresh black pepper	fresh black pepper
250 ml/8 fl oz dry white wine	1 cup dry white wine
Sauce:	*Sauce:*
2 egg yolks	2 egg yolks
juice of ½ lemon	juice of ½ lemon
300 ml/½ pint vegetable oil	1¼ cups vegetable oil
1 × 200 g/7 oz can tuna fish	1 × 7 oz can tuna
4 anchovy fillets	4 anchovy fillets
1 tablespoon capers	1 tablespoon capers
To garnish:	*For garnish:*
1 tablespoon capers	1 tablespoon capers
4 anchovy fillets	4 anchovy fillets
1 tablespoon chopped parsley	1 tablespoon chopped parsley

Place the chicken breasts in a saucepan with the onion, bay leaf, lemon rind, salt, pepper and wine. Cover and cook gently for about 20 minutes or until the chicken is tender.

Meanwhile make the sauce. Using the *Steel Blade*, beat together the egg yolks and lemon juice. With the motor running, gradually add the oil in a thin stream down the feed tube and continue processing for about 1 minute until the mixture is thick and creamy. Add the tuna and anchovies and process again until smooth, then add the capers and, using the on/off or pulse switch, process until well mixed. Do not overprocess or you will chop the capers.

Drain the chicken breasts, reserving the cooking liquid, and arrange them on a serving platter. Thin the tuna sauce if necessary with a little of the cooking liquid, then spoon over the chicken breasts and chill until ready to serve. Serve garnished with capers, anchovies and parsley. Serves 4.

Chicken and Avocado Quiche

Metric/Imperial	American
250 g/8 oz Shortcrust Pastry (see page 25)	½ lb Basic Pie Dough (see page 25)
25 g/1 oz butter	2 tablespoons butter
1 onion, peeled	1 onion, peeled
250 g/8 oz cooked chicken	½ lb cooked chicken
1 avocado	1 avocado
125 g/4 oz herb-flavoured full fat soft cheese	½ cup herb-flavored cream cheese
3 eggs	3 eggs
300 ml/½ pint single cream	1¼ cups light cream
salt	salt
fresh black pepper	fresh black pepper
avocado slices to garnish	avocado sliced for garnish

Roll out the shortcrust pastry (basic pie dough) and use to line a loose-bottomed (spring-form) 23 cm/9 inch flan tin (pan). Line with greaseproof (waxed) paper or foil, add baking beans and bake 'blind' in a preheated moderately hot oven (190°C/375°F, Gas Mark 5) for 10 minutes. Remove the paper and the beans.

Melt the butter in a large frying pan (skillet). Using the *Steel Blade*, finely chop the onion, then sauté in the butter for 3 to 4 minutes. Scatter over the flan case. Still using the *Steel Blade*, chop the chicken into small even-sized pieces, then scatter over the onion in the pastry case. Using the *Shredding Plate* or the *Chip Plate*, shred the avocado and add to the other ingredients in the pastry case with spoonfuls of the cheese. Beat together the eggs, cream, salt and pepper and pour over the other ingredients in the pastry case.

Return to the oven for 35 minutes or until the filling is set and golden. Serve either warm or at room temperature, garnished with avocado slices. Serves 6.

DO leave your food processor assembled and standing on a work surface – you will not make the most use of it if it is tucked away in a cupboard, but wherever you keep your food processor do make sure you keep the blades out of reach of children.

Zested Bacon and Veal Paupiettes

These delicate bacon rolls are filled with a basil-flavoured
veal filling and topped with a creamy lemon sauce.

Metric/Imperial
500 g/1 lb boned veal
    shoulder, cubed
125 g/4 oz white
    breadcrumbs
1 egg white
grated rind of 1 lemon
4 tablespoons chopped
    basil or marjoram
salt
fresh black pepper
8 rashers prime back
    bacon
Sauce:
2 tablespoons oil
25 g/1 oz butter
juice of 1 lemon
300 ml/½ pint chicken
    stock
1 teaspoon cornflour
4 tablespoons single cream
1 egg yolk
To garnish:
lemon wedges
fresh basil sprigs

American
1 lb boneless veal for stew
2 cups white bread crumbs
1 egg white
grated rind of 1 lemon
4 tablespoons chopped
    basil or marjoram
salt
fresh black pepper
8 slices Canadian bacon
Sauce:
2 tablespoons oil
2 tablespoons butter
juice of 1 lemon
1¼ cups chicken stock
1 teaspoon cornstarch
¼ cup light cream
1 egg yolk
For garnish:
lemon wedges
fresh basil sprigs

Using the *Steel Blade*, process the veal until well minced
(ground). Add the breadcrumbs, egg white, lemon rind,
herb, salt and pepper and process again until well mixed.
Divide the mixture into eight parts and roll each into a ball,
then flatten slightly. Wrap each pattie with a rasher (slice)
of bacon and secure with a wooden cocktail stick (tooth-
pick).

Heat the oil and butter in a large frying pan (skillet) and
sauté the paupiettes for 2 to 3 minutes on each side, until
golden. Add the lemon juice, stock and additional salt and
pepper if desired. Cover and simmer for 15-20 minutes.

Transfer the paupiettes to a serving dish and keep warm. Mix the cornflour (cornstarch), cream and egg yolk to form a smooth paste. Add a little of the stock from the pan, stirring. Return this mixture to the pan and heat gently, stirring, until a creamy sauce is formed. Pour over the paupiettes and garnish with the lemon wedges and basil sprigs. Serve with boiled noodles and a green salad. Serves 4.

Zested Veal and Bacon Paupiettes (Pork Farms)

Shellfish Salad With Tarragon

Metric/Imperial	*American*
500 g/1 lb hake or halibut	1 lb hake or halibut
juice of 1½ lemons	juice of 1½ lemons
6 giant prawns, peeled	6 jumbo shrimp, shelled
6 scallops	6 scallops
1 cos lettuce, leaves separated and washed	1 head romaine lettuce, leaves separated and washed
1 green pepper, cored and seeded	1 green pepper, seeded
½ cucumber, peeled	½ cucumber, peeled
4 hard-boiled eggs, shelled and halved	4 hard-cooked eggs, shelled and halved
Herb Sauce:	*Herb Sauce:*
125 g/4 oz medium-fat cheese	½ cup ricotta cheese
150 ml/¼ pint buttermilk	⅔ cup buttermilk
3 tarragon sprigs	3 tarragon sprigs
squeeze of lemon juice	squeeze of lemon juice
salt	salt
fresh black pepper	fresh black pepper

Place the hake or halibut into a large saucepan over moderate heat with just enough cold water to cover. Bring to the boil and poach gently until the fish is cooked and flakes easily when tested with a fork. Remove from the heat and allow the fish to cool in the cooking liquid. When cool, drain, reserving the liquid, then remove the skin and bones and break the flesh into large flakes. Pour over the juice of 1 lemon and set aside.

Soak the prawns (shrimp) in cold, slightly salty water for about 10 minutes.

Poach the scallops for 4 to 5 minutes in the cooking liquid from the fish. Drain, discard the liquid, slice and sprinkle the scallops with a little lemon juice and set aside.

Using the *Slicing Plate*, shred the lettuce, then slice the green pepper and cucumber.

Place the lettuce in a large salad bowl and cover with the pepper and cucumber slices, then put the flaked fish in the centre and surround with the hard-boiled eggs. Scatter the prawns and scallops on top.

To make the sauce, fit the processor with the *Steel Blade* and process the cheese, buttermilk and tarragon until well blended. Season to taste with lemon juice, salt and pepper. Pour over the salad and toss well. Serves 4.

Peachy Chicken with Tarragon Sauce

Metric/Imperial	*American*
3 ripe peaches	3 ripe peaches
300 ml/½ pint dry white wine	1¼ cups dry white wine
2 strips lemon rind	2 strips lemon rind
1 tablespoon chopped fresh tarragon	1 tablespoon chopped fresh tarragon
salt	salt
fresh black pepper	fresh black pepper
4 chicken breasts	4 chicken breasts
a little chicken stock	a little chicken stock
150 ml/¼ pint soured cream	⅔ cup sour cream
To garnish:	*For garnish:*
fresh peach slices	fresh peach slices
a few tarragon sprigs	a few tarragon sprigs

Plunge the peaches into a bowl of boiling water and leave for about 1 minute, then lift out and slip off the skins.

Halve the peaches and remove the stones (pits). Roughly chop the flesh and place in a saucepan with the wine, lemon rind, tarragon, and salt and pepper to taste. Simmer for about 10 minutes or until tender. Allow to cool slightly, then using the *Steel Blade*, process the peaches and the cooking liquid until smooth. Allow to cool in the processor bowl.

Meanwhile, place the chicken breasts in a large frying pan (skillet), with just enough stock to cover. Poach until tender, then skin and set aside to cool. Reserve the cooking liquid. Arrange the breasts on a serving dish.

Blend the soured cream into the peach purée, adding a little of the chicken cooking liquid if necessary to thin the sauce. Pour the sauce over the chicken breasts, cover and chill. To serve, garnish with the peach slices and tarragon sprigs. Serves 4.

Desserts

Damson and Pear Oaty Crumble

Damson and Pear Oaty Crumble

Metric/Imperial	American
125 g/4 oz plain flour	1 cup all-purpose flour
½ teaspoon ground cinnamon	½ teaspoon cinnamon
75 g/3 oz margarine, cubed	6 tablespoons margarine, cubed
75 g/3 oz demerara sugar	6 tablespoons brown sugar
40 g/1½ oz rolled oats	½ cup rolled oats
Filling:	*Filling:*
500 g/1 lb fresh damsons or 1×425 g/15 oz can	1 lb fresh damsons or 1×15 oz can
1 pear, peeled, cored and sliced	1 pear, peeled, cored and sliced
finely grated rind of 1 orange	finely grated rind of 1 orange
2 tablespoons sugar	2 tablespoons sugar

For the topping, place the flour and cinnamon into the processor bowl fitted with the *Steel Blade*, then process for a second or two to sift and mix. Add pieces of the margarine down the feed tube and process until the mixture resembles fine breadcrumbs. Do not overprocess. Add the brown sugar and oats and, using the on/off or pulse switch, process until just mixed.

Place the fruit, orange rind and sugar in a greased 1.2 litre/2 pint (5 cup) ovenproof dish and cover with the crumble topping. Bake in a preheated moderate oven (180°C/350°F, Gas Mark 4) for 30 to 35 minutes or until the filling is soft and the topping golden. Serve with custard or ice cream. Serves 4.

Strawberry Ice Cream

Metric/Imperial	*American*
300 ml/½ pint double cream	1¼ cups heavy cream
500 g/1 lb strawberries, hulled	1 lb strawberries, hulled
250 g/8 oz icing sugar	2 cups confectioners' sugar
sponge finger biscuits to serve	lady fingers for serving

Using the *Plastic Blade* or *Whisk Attachment*, whip the cream. Remove from the processor and reserve. Using the *Metal Blade*, process the strawberries until smooth. Strain through a fine nylon sieve to remove the pips, then stir in the icing (confectioners') sugar. Fold in the cream.

Pour into a freezer tray, cover and freeze until solid. To serve, transfer to the refrigerator for 30 minutes to soften, then serve with sponge finger biscuits (lady fingers). Serves 4.

Variations:
Use raspberries, blackberries or lightly stewed red or black currants instead of the strawberries.

Helpful Hint
When making cakes and whisking cream or egg whites, always leave the food pusher out of the feed tube so air can be drawn down the tube into the mixture.

Blackcurrant and Orange Ice Cream

Metric/Imperial	American
250 g/8 oz blackcurrants, stalks removed	2 cups blackcurrants, stems removed
grated rind and juice of 1 orange	grated rind and juice of 1 orange
6-8 mint leaves	6-8 mint leaves
4 tablespoons soft brown sugar	4 tablespoons soft brown sugar
300 ml/½ pint plain yogurt	1¼ cups plain yogurt
2 eggs, separated	2 eggs, separated
4-6 mint sprigs to decorate	4-6 mint sprigs for decoration

Place the blackcurrants in the processor fitted with the *Steel Blade*, reserving a few for decoration. Add the orange rind and juice, mint leaves, sugar, yogurt and egg yolks; process until smooth. Transfer to a freezer container, cover and freeze until beginning to thicken. Return to the processor and process, using the on/off or pulse switch, until slushy.

Whisk the egg whites until stiff, then fold into the ice cream, using the on/off or pulse switch. Do not over-process. Return to the freezer until half frozen, then beat again, using the *Steel Blade*, to prevent ice crystals forming. Return to the freezer to freeze completely.

To serve, soften in the refrigerator for 20 minutes, then spoon into individual dishes and decorate with the reserved blackcurrants and mint sprigs. Serves 4 to 6.

Pineapple Whip

Metric/Imperial	American
1 ripe pineapple	1 ripe pineapple
about 50 g/2 oz sugar	¼ cup sugar
3 tablespoons kirsch or brandy	3 tablespoons kirsch or brandy
about 500 ml/18 fl oz soft-scoop vanilla ice cream	2 cups soft scoop vanilla ice cream
2 tablespoons chopped walnuts to decorate	2 tablespoons chopped walnuts for decoration

Cut the skin from the pineapple with a sharp knife or breadsaw, then cut 6 neat slices from the centre of the fruit. Discard central cores, then wrap in plastic wrap and reserve.

Remove the core from the remaining pineapple, cut into chunks and, using the *Steel Blade*, process with the sugar and kirsch or brandy. Leave to stand for about 15 minutes to allow the flavours to blend.

Add the ice cream to the pineapple mixture in the processor and, using the on/off or pulse switch, process until well blended. Pour the mixture into a freezer tray, cover and freeze until required.

To serve, arrange the pineapple slices on a serving plate. Spoon the pineapple ice cream on top and sprinkle with chopped nuts. Serves 6.

Dark Chocolate Sauce

Metric/Imperial	*American*
50 g/2 oz plain chocolate, chilled	2 squares semi-sweet chocolate, chilled
150 ml/¼ pint milk or single cream	⅔ cup milk or light cream
125 g/4 oz sugar	½ cup sugar
2 tablespoons cocoa powder	2 tablespoons unsweetened chocolate powder
25 g/1 oz butter	2 tablespoons butter
few drops of vanilla essence	few drops of vanilla

Using the *Shredding Plate*, grate the chocolate. Leave in the bowl. Replace the plate with the *Steel Blade*.

Heat the milk, sugar, cocoa powder (unsweetened chocolate powder) and butter in a saucepan and bring to the boil. With the motor running, pour the mixture down the feed tube into the bowl. Process with the chocolate until well mixed. Return this mixture to the pan and bring to the boil, stirring. Reduce the heat and simmer gently for about 10 minutes, stirring occasionally. Stir in the vanilla essence. Serve hot or cold over ice cream, sponge puddings or fruit. This sauce keeps well; store in an airtight container and refrigerate for up to 1 month. Serves 6.

Five Minute Cheesecake

Metric/Imperial	American
125 ml/4 fl oz whipping cream	½ cup whipping cream
250 g/8 oz full-fat soft cheese	1 cup cream cheese
2 tablespoons icing sugar	2 tablespoons confectioners' sugar
grated rind and juice of 2 oranges	grated rind and juice of 2 oranges
1 × 10-inch sponge flan case	1 × 10-inch sponge flan case
2 oranges to decorate	2 oranges for decoration

Whip the cream in the processor fitted with the *Plastic Blade*. Remove and reserve.

Using the *Steel Blade*, process the cream cheese, icing (confectioners') sugar and orange rind and juice. When smooth, fold in the whipped cream, using the on/off or pulse switch, until just combined. Do not overprocess.

Place the cheesecake mixture into the flan case and smooth the surface.

Cut the rind and pith from the remaining 2 oranges and cut into the membranes to free the segments. Arrange around the cheesecake. Chill for at least 1 hour before serving. Serves 6.

Orange and Treacle Sponge

Metric/Imperial	American
3 tablespoons golden syrup	3 tablespoons light corn syrup
grated rind and juice of 2 oranges	grated rind and juice of 2 oranges
1 slice white bread, cubed	1 slice white bread, cubed
125 g/4 oz butter	½ cup butter
125 g/4 oz sugar	½ cup sugar
2 eggs	2 eggs
125 g/4 oz self-raising flour	1 cup self-rising flour
1 teaspoon baking powder	1 teaspoon baking powder
grated rind and juice of 1 lemon	grated rind and juice of 1 lemon

Orange and Treacle Sponge (Summer Orange Office)

Place the syrup, orange rind and juice in a saucepan over moderate heat and heat gently. Fit the processor with the *Steel Blade* and drop the bread cubes down the feed tube, processing until fine breadcrumbs are formed. Add to the syrup mixture and stir to mix. Remove and reserve. Still using the *Steel Blade*, make up the sponge with the butter, sugar, eggs, flour and baking powder, using the method on page 32. Add the lemon rind and juice and process with the on/off or pulse switch until just mixed.

Pour the syrup and orange mixture into a greased 900 ml/1½ pint (3¾ cup) pudding basin (heatproof mixing bowl) and spoon the sponge mixture on top. Cover with a double layer of greaseproof (waxed) paper, then foil, securing the edges well. Steam over simmering water for about 1 hour. Invert on to a serving plate and serve with vanilla ice cream or custard. Serves 4-6.

Danish Apple Cakes

Metric/Imperial	American
750 g/1½ lb cooking apples, peeled and cored	1½ lb tart apples, pared and cored
75 g/3 oz butter	6 tablespoons butter
4 slices white bread, cubed	4 slices white bread, cubed
75 g/3 oz sugar	6 tablespoons sugar
sugar to taste (optional)	sugar to taste (optional)
150 ml/¼ pint whipping cream	⅔ cup whipping cream
redcurrant jelly to decorate	redcurrant jelly for decoration

Using the *Slicing Plate*, slice the apples in the processor. Remove from the bowl and place in a saucepan over moderate heat with just enough water to cover and one-third of the butter. Cover and simmer until soft.

Meanwhile, using the *Steel Blade*, process the bread to form fine breadcrumbs. Heat the remaining butter in a frying pan (skillet) and add the sugar and the crumbs. Cook gently for 20 minutes or until golden, stirring occasionally. Remove from the heat and set aside to cool completely.

Transfer the apples to the processor fitted with the *Steel Blade* and purée until smooth, adding a little extra sugar to taste if liked. Just before serving, arrange alternate layers of apple purée (apple sauce) and crumbs in four individual glass dishes, finishing with a layer of crumbs.

Clean the bowl and fit with the *Plastic Blade* or *Whisk Attachment* and whip the cream. Spread over the top of each portion and top with redcurrant jelly. Serves 4.

Minted Apple Snow

Metric/Imperial	American
1 kg/2 lb cooking apples, peeled and cored	2 lb tart apples, pared and cored
finely grated rind and juice of 1 orange	finely grated rind and juice of 1 orange
3 tablespoons clear honey	3 tablespoons clear honey
4 large mint sprigs	4 large mint sprigs
2 large egg whites	2 large egg whites

Using the *Slicing Plate*, slice the apples, then place in a large saucepan over moderate heat with the orange rind and juice, honey and mint sprigs, reserving a few leaves for decoration. Cover and cook gently for about 15 minutes, stirring occasionally, until the apples are reduced to a pulp. Remove the mint.

Fit the processor with the *Steel Blade* and process the apple mixture until smooth. Leave to cool in the bowl.

Whisk the egg whites until stiff, then fold into the apple purée using the on/off or pulse switch.

Spoon into a glass serving bowl or individual dishes and decorate with the reserved mint leaves. Chill until ready to serve. Serves 4.

Soured Cream Peach Tart

Metric/Imperial	*American*
250 g/8 oz plain flour	2 cups all-purpose flour
pinch of salt	pinch of salt
pinch of baking powder	pinch of baking powder
200 g/7 oz sugar	¾ cup plus 2 tablespoons
125 g/4 oz butter, diced	sugar
1×825 g/1¾ lb can peach	½ cup butter, diced
halves, drained	1×1¾ lb can peach
1 teaspoon ground	halves, drained
cinnamon	1 teaspoon cinnamon
250 ml/8 fl oz soured cream	1 cup sour cream
2 egg yolks	2 egg yolks

Place the flour, salt, baking powder and 2 tablespoons of the sugar in the processor fitted with the *Steel Blade* and sift, using the on/off or pulse switch. Add the butter down the feed tube and process until the mixture resembles fine breadcrumbs. Do not overprocess. Press the mixture on to the base and half way up the side of a 25 cm/10 inch loose-bottomed (springform) cake tin (pan).

Arrange the peach halves in the pastry case (pie shell), then sprinkle with the cinnamon and remaining sugar. Beat together the soured cream and egg yolks and pour over the peaches. Bake in a preheated moderately hot oven (200°C/400°F, Gas Mark 6) for about 30 minutes or until golden. Serves 8.

Cakes and Biscuits (Cookies)

Treacle Tart

Metric/Imperial
1 quantity Shortcrust
    Pastry (see page 25)
2 slices white bread, cubed
250 g/8 oz golden syrup
grated rind of 1 lemon
juice of ½ lemon

American
1 quantity Basic Pie Dough
    (see page 25)
2 slices white bread, cubed
¾ cup light corn syrup
grated rind of 1 lemon
juice of ½ lemon

Use the pastry to line a 20 cm/8 inch shallow pie plate. Trim the edges and reserve the pastry trimmings.

Using the *Steel Blade*, process the bread until fine crumbs form, then transfer to a saucepan over moderate heat with the syrup, lemon rind and juice. Heat gently, stirring, until the syrup is runny, then pour into the pastry case (pie shell).

Decorate the top with a lattice (trellis) pattern of pastry strips cut from the trimmings. Bake in a preheated moderate oven (180°C/350°F, Gas Mark 4) for 30 minutes or until the pastry is golden. Serve warm with cream or ice cream. Serves 4 to 6.

Treacle Tart

All-In-One Walnut Fudge Cake

Metric/Imperial	American
50 g/2 oz walnuts	½ cup walnuts
125 g/4 oz margarine	½ cup margarine
125 g/4 oz caster sugar	½ cup superfine sugar
1 tablespoon golden syrup	1 tablespoon light corn
2 eggs, beaten	syrup
175 g/6 oz self-raising flour	2 eggs, beaten
½ teaspoon baking powder	1½ cups self rising flour
2 tablespoons strong black	½ teaspoon baking powder
coffee	2 tablespoons strong black
walnut halves to decorate	coffee
Fudge Icing:	walnut halves to decorate
150 ml/¼ pint milk	*Fudge Frosting:*
100 g/4 oz soft brown sugar	⅔ cup milk
25 g/1 oz margarine	⅔ cup firmly packed soft light
few drops of vanilla	brown sugar
essence	2 tablespoons margarine
	few drops of vanilla

Thoroughly grease and flour two 18 cm/7 inch round sandwich loose-bottomed (springform) cake tins (pans). Using the *Steel Blade*, chop the walnuts. Remove and reserve. Place the remaining cake ingredients in the bowl and process until well mixed. Add the nuts, and, using the on/off or pulse switch, process until they have been folded into the mixture.

Spoon the mixture into the prepared tins (pans). Bake in a preheated moderate oven (180°C/350°F, Gas Mark 4) for about 20 minutes. Invert on to a wire rack to cool completely. When cold, split in half horizontally.

To make the icing (frosting), place the milk, sugar, margarine and vanilla in a saucepan over a low heat and stir gently until the margarine melts and the sugar dissolves. Bring to the boil, then boil for 5 minutes. Pour the mixture into the food processor, fitted with the *Steel Blade*, and process until it thickens. Spread half the icing over one layer of the cake, then sandwich the two layers together. Spread the remaining icing (frosting) over the top and decorate with the walnut halves. Makes one 18 cm/7 inch round cake.

Chilled Fruit and Nut Cheesecake

Metric/Imperial	American
175 g/6 oz digestive biscuits, roughly broken	1½ cups roughly broken graham crackers
50 g/2 oz hazelnuts or walnuts	½ cup hazelnuts or walnuts
125 g/4 oz butter	½ cup butter
Filling:	*Filling:*
1 × 350 g/12 oz can mandarin oranges or fruit of your choice	1 × ¾ lb can mandarin oranges or fruit of your choice
1 tablespoon gelatine	1 tablespoon gelatin
finely grated rind and juice of 1 lemon	finely grated rind and juice of 1 lemon
350 g/12 oz full-fat soft cheese	1½ cups cream cheese
75 g/3 oz sugar	6 tablespoons sugar
150 ml/¼ pint soured cream	⅔ cup sour cream
2 eggs, separated	2 eggs, separated

Fit the processor with the *Steel Blade*. Drop the biscuits and nuts down the feed tube and process to fine crumbs.

Melt the butter in a saucepan over moderate heat, then stir in the chopped biscuit mixture. Press into the base of a greased loose-bottomed (springform) 20 cm/8 inch tin (pan). Refrigerate until required.

To make the filling, drain the mandarins, reserving 150 ml/¼ pint (⅔ cup) of the juice; pour into a small heatproof bowl. Sprinkle the gelatine over and leave for a few minutes, until spongy. Stand the bowl in a pan of hot water and heat gently, stirring, until the gelatine dissolves. Remove from the heat and stir in the lemon rind and juice.

Using the *Steel Blade*, process the cheese and sugar until creamy. With the motor running, add the soured cream and egg yolks down the feed tube, followed by the gelatine mixture.

Whisk the whites until stiff, then carefully fold into the cheese mixture, using the on/off or pulse switch. Be careful not to overprocess. Pour the mixture into the biscuit-lined pan and refrigerate for 3 hours, until set.

To serve, remove the cheesecake from the tin (pan), place on a serving platter and decorate with the reserved fruit. Serves 8.

White Fruit Cake

Metric/Imperial	*American*
50 g/2 oz Brazil nuts	1/2 cup Brazil nuts
50 g/2 oz blanched almonds	1/2 cup blanched almonds
50 g/2 oz glacé cherries	1/4 cup candied cherries
50 g/2 oz glacé pineapple	1/4 cup candied pineapple
200 g/7 oz plain flour	3/4 cup all-purpose flour
175 g/6 oz butter	3/4 cup butter
175 g/6 oz icing sugar, sifted	1 1/3 cups sifted confectioners' sugar
3 eggs	3 eggs
1/2 teaspoon vanilla essence	1/2 teaspoon vanilla
150 g/5 oz sultanas	1 cup golden raisins

Grease a 1 kg/2 lb (4 cup) loaf tin (pan) and line with greaseproof (waxed) paper. Using the *Steel Blade*, process the nuts until roughly chopped. Reserve. Toss the cherries and pineapple in a little flour, add to the processor and roughly chop. Reserve.

Place the butter in the processor and process until creamy, then, with the motor running, add the sugar down the feed tube and process until well creamed. Add the eggs, one at a time down the feed tube, then add the vanilla essence. Remove the processor lid and add the reserved nuts and fruit, sultanas (golden raisins) and flour. Using the on/off or pulse switch, process until the mixture is blended, but do not overmix. Transfer the mixture to the prepared tin (pan) and bake in a preheated cool oven (150°C/300°F, Gas Mark 2) for 1 hour. Reduce the oven temperature to 140°C/275°F, Gas Mark 1, and bake for a further hour or until a skewer inserted in the centre of the cake comes out clean. Invert on to a wire rack to cool completely. Remove the paper when the cake is cold, then store in an airtight container until ready to serve. Makes one 1 kg/2 lb cake.

*Chocolate Crunch Gâteau
(New Zealand Kiwifruit)*

Chocolate Crunch Gâteau

Metric/Imperial	*American*
250 g/8 oz dates, stoned	1½ cups dates, pitted
300 g/10 oz plain chocolate, broken into pieces	10 oz semi-sweet chocolate, broken into pieces
75 g/3 oz butter	⅓ cup butter
12 sponge fingers, roughly chopped	12 lady fingers, roughly chopped
1 large banana	1 large banana
juice of 1 lime	juice of 1 lime
25 g/1 oz icing sugar, sifted	¼ cup confectioners' sugar, sifted
600 ml/1 pint double cream, whipped	2½ cups heavy cream, whipped
125 g/4 oz strawberries, chopped	1 cup strawberries, chopped
2 kiwifruits, chopped	2 kiwifruits, chopped
1 sliced kiwifruit to decorate	1 sliced kiwifruit to decorate

Grease and line two 20 cm/8 inch sandwich tins (pans). Using the *Steel Blade*, chop the dates and reserve.

Place the broken chocolate and butter in a bowl together over a pan of hot water and stir to melt. Mix the dates with the chopped fingers. When the chocolate mixture has melted, pour over the date mixture and mix well. Divide between the two tins (pans) and spread evenly. Chill to set.

Using the *Steel Blade*, mash the banana with the lime juice and icing (confectioners') sugar. Using the on/off or pulse switch, fold in the cream and chopped fruits.

Invert the set cakes and remove the lining paper from the bases. Place one cake on a serving plate and carefully cut the other into 8 pieces. Pile the cream mixture on to the base and arrange the cut cake on the top. Decorate with kiwifruit slices and serve. Makes one 20 cm/8 inch cake.

Chocolate and Cherry Crumb Cake

Metric/Imperial	*American*
125 g/4 oz soft tub margarine	½ cup margarine
2 tablespoons sugar	2 tablespoons sugar
2 tablespoons cocoa powder	2 tablespoons unsweetened chocolate powder
2 tablespoons golden syrup	2 tablespoons light corn syrup
250 g/8 oz digestive biscuits, roughly broken	4 cups roughly broken graham crackers
50 g/2 oz glacé cherries	⅓ cup candied cherries
Icing:	*Frosting:*
75 g/3 oz icing sugar	6 tablespoons confectioners' sugar
2 tablespoons cocoa powder	2 tablespoons unsweetened chocolate powder
3 tablespoons water	3 tablespoons water

Place all the cake ingredients in the processor fitted with the *Steel Blade*. Process until the biscuits are finely crushed and the ingredients well mixed. Press into a greased loose-bottomed (springform) 20 cm/8 inch cake tin (pan) and refrigerate for about 2 hours, until firm.

To make the icing (frosting), place all the ingredients in the processor bowl fitted with the *Plastic Blade* and process until smooth. Spread over the cake and allow to set. Cut into slices to serve. Makes one 20 cm/8 inch cake.

Foolproof Chocolate Cake

Metric/Imperial	American
150 g/5 oz plain flour	1 cup plus 2 tablespoons all-purpose flour
2 teaspoons baking powder	2 teaspoons baking powder
4 tablespoons cocoa powder	4 tablespoons unsweetened chocolate powder
8 tablespoons boiling water	1/2 cup boiling water
4 tablespoons oil	1/4 cup oil
4 eggs	4 eggs
175 g/6 oz sugar	2/3 cup sugar
1 teaspoon vanilla essence	1 teaspoon vanilla

Grease and flour two 20 cm/8 inch sandwich cake tins
(layer cake pans). Place the flour and baking powder in the
bowl fitted with the *Steel Blade* and process for one second
to sift. Reserve. Dissolve the cocoa in the water, then add
the oil and set aside. Place one egg and three yolks in the
food processor and beat until frothy. With the motor running, gradually add the sugar down the feed tube and
continue processing for about 1 minute. Add the cocoa
mixture and the vanilla, then the sifted flour down the feed
tube. Process until well beaten. Whisk the remaining three
egg whites until stiff, spoon on to the cake mixture in the
bowl and, using the on/off or pulse switch, fold into the
chocolate mixture. Be careful not to overprocess.

Pour into the prepared tins (pans) and bake in a preheated moderately hot oven (200°C/400°F, Gas Mark 6)
for 25 minutes. Invert on to a wire rack to cool, then
sandwich the two layers together with butter icing or whipped double (heavy) cream. Make one 20 cm/8 inch cake.

Instant Orange Frosting

Metric/Imperial	American
2 tablespoons frozen orange concentrate	2 tablespoons frozen orange concentrate
40 g/1 1/2 oz soft margarine	3 tablespoons margarine
175 g/6 oz icing sugar, sifted	1 1/2 cups sifted confectioners' sugar

Place all the ingredients in the processor fitted with the *Steel Blade* and process until smooth. Stop and scrape down the processor bowl if necessary. Makes enough to fill and coat the top of an 18 cm/7 inch sandwich (layer) cake.
Variation:
Coffee Frosting: Use 2 tablespoons coffee essence (extract) instead of orange concentrate.

Spice Cake

Metric/Imperial	*American*
250 g/8 oz self-raising flour	2 cups self-rising flour
1 teaspoon baking powder	1 teaspoon baking powder
pinch of salt	pinch of salt
pinch of ground clove	pinch of ground clove
pinch of nutmeg	pinch of nutmeg
½ teaspoon allspice	½ teaspoon allspice
½ teaspoon ground cinnamon	½ teaspoon cinnamon
175 g/6 oz butter	¾ cup butter
175 g/6 oz sugar	¾ cup sugar
3 eggs, beaten	3 eggs, beaten
150 ml/¼ pint plain yogurt	⅔ cup plain yogurt
50 g/2 oz ground almonds	½ cup ground almonds
1 tablespoon boiling water	1 tablespoon boiling water
100 g/4 oz raisins	⅔ cup raisins

Grease and line an 18 cm/7 inch round cake tin (pan). Place the flour, baking powder, salt and spices in the processor with the *Steel Blade* fitted and turn on for one second to sift. Set aside.

Place the butter and sugar in the processor and process until creamed, then add the eggs and yogurt and process until well blended. Add the flour mixture and the almonds and process until just mixed, then add the boiling water and fold in the raisins. Spoon the mixture into the prepared tin (pan) and smooth the surface.

Bake in a preheated moderate oven (160°C/325°F, Gas Mark 3) for 1¼ hours, until a skewer inserted in the centre comes out clean. Cool the cake for 15 minutes in the tin (pan), then invert on to a wire rack to cool completely. Makes one 18 cm/7 inch cake.

Pickles and Preserves

Chutneys

Pear and Ginger Chutney

Metric/Imperial	American
2.75 kg/6 lb pears, peeled and cored	6 lb pears, peeled and cored
500 g/1 lb onions, peeled	1 lb onions, peeled
125 g/4 oz stem ginger	¼ lb preserved ginger
25 g/1 oz root ginger, roughly chopped	2 tablespoons roughly chopped ginger root
1 teaspoon cloves	1 teaspoon cloves
grated rind and juice of 3 oranges	grated rind and juice of 3 oranges
750 g/1½ lb sugar	3 cups sugar
900 ml/1½ pints red wine vinegar	3¾ cups red wine vinegar

Using the *Steel Blade*, chop the pears, onions and stem ginger (preserved ginger) in individual batches, then place in a large stainless steel, aluminium or enamelled pan. Tie the root ginger and cloves in a muslin (cheesecloth) bag, then add to the pan with the remaining ingredients. Stir over a low heat until the sugar dissolves. Bring to the boil, then reduce the heat and simmer for 1½ hours or until the chutney is thick.

Remove the muslin bag and spoon the hot chutney into warm, dry, sterilized jars. Seal with airtight, vinegar-proof covers and label. Leave for 2 to 3 months before using. Makes about 1.75 kg/4 lb.

Mediterranean Chutney

Metric/Imperial	*American*
1 kg/2 lb tomatoes, skinned	2 lb tomatoes, peeled
500 g/1 lb Spanish onions, peeled	1 lb Spanish onions, peeled
2 large cloves garlic, peeled	2 large cloves garlic, peeled
500 g/1 lb courgettes	1 lb zucchini
1 large green pepper, cored and seeded	1 large green pepper, seeded
1 large red pepper, cored and seeded	1 large red pepper, seeded
250 g/8 oz aubergine	½ lb eggplant
1 tablespoon salt	1 tablespoon salt
1 tablespoon cayenne pepper	1 tablespoon cayenne
1 tablespoon paprika	1 tablespoon paprika
1 tablespoon ground coriander	1 tablespoon ground coriander
300 ml/½ pint malt vinegar	1¼ cups malt vinegar
350 g/12 oz sugar	1½ cups sugar

Using the *Steel Blade*, chop the tomatoes, Spanish onions and garlic in individual batches, then place in a large stainless steel, aluminium or enamelled pan. Using the *Slicing Blade*, slice the courgettes (zucchini), green and red peppers and aubergine (eggplant) in individual batches, then add to the pan with the salt, cayenne, paprika and coriander.

Cover and cook gently, stirring occasionally, until the juices run. Bring to the boil, then reduce the heat, uncover and simmer for 1 to 1½ hours or until the vegetables are tender but still firm and most of the liquid has evaporated.

Add the vinegar and sugar, stirring to dissolve the sugar. Continue to cook for a further 1 hour, until the chutney is thick and there is no vinegar floating on the surface.

Spoon the hot chutney into warm, dry, sterilized jars. Seal with airtight, vinegar-proof covers and label. Leave for 2 to 3 months before using. Makes about 1.75 kg/4 lb.

Mint Chutney

Metric/Imperial	American
1 kg/2 lb cooking apples, peeled and cored	2 lb tart apples, pared and cored
1 kg/2 lb onions, peeled	2 lb onions, peeled
500 g/1 lb tomatoes, skinned	1 lb tomatoes, peeled
8 sprigs mint	8 sprigs mint
4 sprigs parsley	4 sprigs parsley
250 g/8 oz sultanas	1⅓ cups golden raisins
grated rind and juice of 2 lemons	grated rind and juice of 2 lemons
600 ml/1 pint cider vinegar	2½ cups cider vinegar
500 g/1 lb sugar	2 cups sugar
2 teaspoons salt	2 teaspoons salt

Using the *Steel Blade*, chop the apples, onions, tomatoes, mint and parsley in individual batches, then transfer to a large stainless steel, aluminium or enamelled pan with the remaining ingredients. Stir over a low heat until the sugar dissolves. Bring to the boil, then reduce the heat and cook gently, stirring occasionally, for about 1½ hours or until the fruit is reduced to a pulp and the chutney is thick.

Spoon the hot chutney into warm, dry, sterilized jars. Seal with airtight, vinegar-proof covers and label. Leave for 2 to 3 months before using. Makes about 2 kg/4½ lb.

Cucumber Pickle

Metric/Imperial	American
1 kg/2 lb cucumbers	2 lb cucumbers
2 onions, peeled	2 onions, peeled
1 green pepper, quartered, cored and seeded	1 green pepper, quartered and seeded
3 tablespoons salt	3 tablespoons salt
450 ml/¾ pint cider vinegar	2 cups cider vinegar
250 g/8 oz sugar	1 cup sugar
2 tablespoons mustard seed	2 tablespoons mustard seed
1 teaspoon ground ginger	1 teaspoon ground ginger

Using the *Steel Blade*, slice the cucumbers, onions and pepper in individual batches. Place in a bowl and sprinkle with the salt. Cover and set aside for 12 hours to extract the moisture. Rinse the vegetables well to remove the salt, then drain and pat dry.

Place the vinegar in a large saucepan with the remaining ingredients and heat slowly until the sugar dissolves, then bring to the boil. Add the vegetables and simmer gently for 5 minutes or until the vegetables are just tender. While still hot, spoon into warm, dry, sterilized jars and cover with the vinegar from the pan. Seal with airtight, vinegar-proof covers and label. Leave for 3 to 4 weeks before using. Makes 2 kg/4½ lb.

Beetroot Chutney

Metric/Imperial	*American*
2 kg/4 lb beetroot, cooked and skinned	4 lb beets, cooked and peeled
1 kg/2 lb cooking apples, peeled and cored	2 lb tart apples, pared and cored
500 g/1 lb onions, peeled	1 lb onions, peeled
grated rind and juice of 2 large lemons	grated rind and juice of 2 large lemons
2 tablespoons grated root ginger or 2 teaspoons ground ginger	2 tablespoons grated ginger root or 2 teaspoons ground ginger
2 teaspoons salt	2 teaspoons salt
1 teaspoon fresh black pepper	1 teaspoon fresh black pepper
1 litre/1¾ pints vinegar	4¼ cups vinegar
500 g/1 lb sugar	2 cups sugar

Using the *Steel Blade*, roughly chop the beetroot, then transfer to a large stainless steel, aluminium or enamelled pan. Finely chop the apples and onions and add to the pan with the remaining ingredients. Stir over a low heat until the sugar dissolves. Bring to the boil, then reduce the heat and simmer for 1½ hours or until the chutney is thick.

Spoon the hot chutney into warm, dry, sterilized jars. Seal with airtight, vinegar-proof covers and label. Leave for 2 to 3 months before using. Makes about 3 kg/6½ lb.

Citrus Marmalade

Metric/Imperial	*American*
1.5 kg/3 lb mixed citrus fruit (about 2 medium grapefruit, 2 medium oranges, 4 medium lemons)	3 lb mixed citrus fruit (about 2 medium grapefruit, 2 medium oranges, 4 medium lemons)
3.5 litres/6 pints water	7½ pints water
2.75 kg/6 lb sugar	12 cups sugar

Wash the fruits and cut each in half. Squeeze out the juice and pour into a large preserving pan. Tie the pips (seeds) in a piece of muslin (cheesecloth) and add to the juice in the pan. Cut the orange and lemon rinds in half again and each piece of the grapefruit rinds into quarters.

Using the *Slicing Blade*, slice the rinds in thick or thin shreds, without removing the pith, then add to the pan.

Pour the water into the pan and bring to the boil. Reduce the heat, then simmer for 1½ hours or until the peel is soft. Remove the bag; squeeze the juice back into the pan.

Add the sugar and stir over a low heat until it dissolves. Boil rapidly until setting point (105°C/220°F) is reached. Remove any scum from the surface. Allow to cool slightly before pouring into warm, dry, sterilized jars. Wipe clean and cover with paper discs, waxed sides down. Allow to cool, then cover with jam pot covers and secure with rubber bands. Label and store for up to 1 year. Makes about 4.5 kg/10 lb.

Tangerine Marmalade

Metric/Imperial	*American*
1 kg/2 lb tangerines	2 lb tangerines
500 g/1 lb lemons	1 lb lemons
3.5 litres/6 pints water	7½ pints water
2.75 kg/6 lb sugar	6 lb sugar

Wash the tangerines and lemons, then cut in half. Squeeze out the juice and pour into a large preserving pan. Tie the pips (seeds) in a piece of muslin (cheesecloth) and add to the juice.

Using the *Slicing Blade*, finely slice the tangerine and lemon rinds without removing the pith, then add to the pan. Pour the water into the pan and bring to the boil. Reduce the heat, then simmer for 1½ hours or until the peel is very soft. Remove the muslin bag, squeezing the juice back into the pan.

Add the sugar and stir over a low heat until it dissolves. Boil rapidly until setting point (105°C/220°F) is reached. Remove any scum from the surface. Allow to cool slightly before pouring into warm, dry, sterilized jars. Wipe clean and cover with paper discs, waxed sides down. Allow to cool, then cover with jam pot covers and secure with rubber bands. Label and store for up to 1 year. Makes about 4.5 kg/10 lb.

Lemon and Honey Marmalade, page 88

Lemon and Honey Marmalade

Metric/Imperial	American
750 g/1½ lb lemons	1½ lb lemons
1.25 kg/2½ lb cooking apples	2½ lb tart apples
3.5 litres/6 pints water	8 pints water
1.75 kg/4 lb sugar	8 cups sugar
1 kg/2 lb clear honey	2 lb clear honey

Wash the lemons and cut in half. Squeeze out the juice, reserving the pips (seeds), and pour into a large preserving pan. Peel, quarter and core the apples, reserving the peel and cores.

Using the *Slicing Blade*, finely slice the lemon rind without removing the pith, then add to the pan. Using the same blade, slice the apples, then add to the pan. Tie the apple peel and cores and the lemon pips in a piece of muslin (cheesecloth) and add to the fruit in the pan.

Pour the water into the pan and bring to the boil. Reduce the heat, then simmer for 1½ hours or until the lemon rind is very soft. Remove the muslin bag, squeezing the juice back into the pan.

Add the sugar and honey and stir over a low heat until the sugar dissolves. Boil rapidly until setting point (105°C/220°F) is reached. Remove any scum from the surface. Allow to cool slightly before pouring into warm, dry, sterilized jars. Wipe clean and cover with paper discs, waxed sides down. Allow to cool, then cover with jam pot covers and secure with rubber bands. Label and store for up to 1 year. Makes about 4.5 kg/10 lb.

Bramble Butter

Metric/Imperial	American
1 kg/2 lb cooking apples, peeled and cored	2 lb tart apples, pared and cored
1 kg/2 lb blackberries	2 lb blackberries
grated rind and juice of 2 lemons	grated rind and juice of 2 lemons
1 kg/2 lb sugar (approximately)	4 cups sugar (approximately)

Fit the processor with the *Steel Blade* and roughly chop the apples. Place in a large saucepan with the blackberries and lemon rind and juice. Cover and cook gently for 15 minutes or until the fruit is soft and pulpy. Remove from the heat and purée in the food processor, using the *Steel Blade*. Weigh the purée.

Return the purée to the pan and add 350 g/12 oz (1½ cups) sugar for each 500 g/1 lb (2 cups) purée. Bring slowly to the boil, stirring, until the sugar dissolves. Continue cooking until the mixture develops a thick, creamy consistency. Pour into warm, dry, sterilized jars or moulds, and cover each with a waxed disc and plastic wrap. Bramble Butter will keep up to 3 months in a cupboard and up to 6 months in the refrigerator. Makes about 1.5 kg/3 lb.

Tomato, Apple and Orange Relish

Metric/Imperial	American
500 g/1 lb tomatoes, skinned	1 lb tomatoes, peeled
500 g/1 lb cooking apples, peeled and cored	1 lb tart apples, pared and cored
500 g/1 lb onions, peeled	1 lb onions, peeled
25 g/1 oz root ginger, peeled	¼-inch piece ginger root, peeled
350 g/12 oz soft brown sugar	2 cups soft brown sugar
300 ml/½ pint cider vinegar or white wine vinegar	1¼ cups cider vinegar or white wine vinegar
grated rind and juice of 2 large oranges	grated rind and juice of 2 large oranges

Using the *Steel Blade*, roughly chop the tomatoes, apples, onions and ginger in individual batches.

Place the sugar, vinegar, orange rind and juice and ginger in a saucepan. Bring to the boil slowly. Add the tomatoes, apples and onions. Simmer, uncovered, for about 30 minutes or until most of the liquid has evaporated. While still hot, spoon into warm, dry, sterilized jars or bottles. Seal with airtight, vinegar-proof covers and label. Store in a cool, dry, dark place. Makes about 1.5 kg/3 lb.

Drinks

Fruity Yogurt Cooler

Metric/Imperial	American
150 g/5 oz ripe strawberries, peaches, apricots or plums, sliced	1 cup sliced ripe strawberries, peaches, apricots or plums
150 ml/¼ pint fruit-flavoured yogurt	⅔ cup fruit-flavored yogurt
250 ml/8 fl oz milk	1 cup milk
sugar	sugar

Have the fruit, yogurt and milk icy cold.

Using the *Steel Blade*, process the fruit to a purée. Using the on/off or pulse switch add the yogurt and milk, mix well. Add sugar to taste. Serves 3.

Tropical Frost

Metric/Imperial	American
450 ml/¾ pint unsweetened pineapple juice	2 cups unsweetened pineapple juice
450 ml/¾ pint orange juice	2 cups orange juice
4 tablespoons lemon juice	¼ cup lemon juice
6 scoops fruit-flavoured ice cream	6 scoops fruit-flavored ice cream
sprigs of mint, to garnish	sprigs of mint, to garnish

Using the *Plastic Blade*, combine the fruit juices and half the ice cream in the processor bowl.

Divide between six glasses. Add a small scoop of ice cream to each and decorate with a sprig of mint. Serves 6.

Apricot Cream

Metric/Imperial	American
6 ripe apricots, stoned	6 ripe apricots, pitted
120 ml/4 fl oz milk	½ cup milk
120 ml/4 fl oz single cream	½ cup light cream
1 tablespoon lemon juice	1 tablespoon lemon juice
2 tablespoons sugar	2 tablespoons sugar
125 g/4 oz ice	½ cup ice

Clockwise from top left: Orange Melon Frost; Apricot Cream; Tropical Frost; Fruity Yogurt Cooler; Lemon Buttermilk Delight, page 92

Using the *Steel Blade*, chop the apricots and crush the ice in individual batches. Place the remaining ingredients in the processor bowl and process until smooth and creamy. Add the apricots and crushed ice and mix well, using the on/off or pulse switch. Pour into tall chilled glasses to serve. Serves 3 to 4.

Orange-Melon Frost

Metric/Imperial
2 medium oranges, peeled and seeded
150 ml/5 oz peeled melon (honeydew, Charentais or watermelon) roughly chopped
2 tablespoons lemon juice
pinch of salt
125 g/4 oz ice, finely crushed

American
2 medium oranges, peeled and seeded
1 cup roughly chopped melon (honeydew, Canteloupe or watermelon)
2 tablespoons lemon juice
pinch of salt
½ cup finely crushed ice

Using the *Steel Blade*, place all the ingredients in the procesor and combine until frothy. Serves 3 to 4.

Lemon Buttermilk Delight

Metric/Imperial	*American*
250 ml/8 fl oz double cream	1 cup heavy cream
1 litre/1¾ pints buttermilk	1 quart buttermilk
2 teaspoons grated lemon rind	2 teaspoons grated lemon rind
4 tablespoons lemon juice	¼ cup lemon juice
125 g/4 oz sugar	½ cup sugar
ground cinnamon	ground cinnamon

Using the *Plastic Blade*, whip the cream until soft peaks form. Set aside.

Still using the *Plastic Blade*, whip the buttermilk with the lemon rind, juice and sugar until frothy. Using the on/off or pulse switch, combine the cream and buttermilk mixture together.

Serve in tall chilled glasses with a sprinkle of cinnamon on top. Serves 6 to 8.

Illustrated on page 91.

Iced Coffee Special

Metric/Imperial	*American*
1 tablespoon instant coffee powder	1 tablespoon instant coffee powder
2 tablespoons boiling water	2 tablespoons boiling water
300 ml/½ pint milk, chilled	1¼ cups chilled milk
4 tablespoons vanilla ice cream	4 tablespoons vanilla ice cream
1 tablespoon sugar (optional)	1 tablespoon sugar (optional)
2 tablespoons brandy	2 tablespoons brandy
ground cinnamon to decorate	ground cinnamon for decoration

Dissolve the coffee in the boiling water and leave to cool. Place the cooled coffee and all the remaining ingredients in the food processor fitted with the *Steel Blade* and process for about 10 seconds. Pour into two tall chilled glasses and serve immediately, sprinkled with a little cinnamon. Serves 2.

Chocolate Mint Cooler

Metric/Imperial	American
300 ml/½ pint milk, chilled	1¼ cups chilled milk
4 teaspoons drinking chocolate	4 teaspoons drinking chocolate
4 tablespoons vanilla ice cream	4 tablespoons vanilla ice cream
a few drops of mint essence	a few drops of mint extract
drinking chocolate to decorate	drinking chocolate for decoration

Place all the ingredients in the processor fitted with the *Steel Blade* and process for about 10 seconds. Pour into two tall glasses and serve immediately, sprinkled with a little drinking chocolate. Serves 2.

Liquid Breakfast

Metric/Imperial	American
150 ml/¼ pint orange juice	⅔ cup fresh orange juice
1 egg	1 egg
150 ml/¼ pint plain yogurt	⅔ cup plain yogurt

Place all the ingredients in the processor fitted with the *Steel Blade*. Process for about 10 seconds and serve immediately. Serves 1.
Variation:
Use grapefruit juice instead of the orange juice. Add clear honey to taste.

Eskimo

Metric/Imperial	American
½ litre/18 fl oz ice cream	2 cups ice cream
150 ml/¼ pint whisky	⅔ cup whisky

Place just under half the ice cream in the processor fitted with the *Steel Blade*. Add the whisky and process until smooth, adding the remaining ice cream gradually down the feed tube. Pour into four chilled glasses and serve with a straw. Serves 4.

Buttermilk and Watercress

Buttermilk and Watercress

Metric/Imperial	*American*
600 ml/1 pint buttermilk	2½ cups buttermilk
150 ml/¼ pint plain yogurt	⅔ cup plain yogurt
1 bunch watercress	1 bunch watercress
2 tablespoons chopped chives	2 tablespoons chopped chives

Purée the buttermilk and yogurt together in the processor fitted with the *Steel Blade*. Add the leaves of the watercress and blend again. Using the on/off or pulse switch stir in the chives and pour into four chilled glasses. Makes 4 small glasses.

Variation:
Mix the buttermilk and yogurt together in the processor. Cut the heads off 2 baskets of cress and add them with 12 young sorrel leaves. Blend again, and pour into four glasses. Garnish with a sprig of mint, if liked. Makes 4 smallish glasses.

Index

Acknowledgments

The publishers would like to thank the following photographers:
Bryce Attwell 15, 19, 38; Robert Golden 34, 91; Melvin Grey 82, 94; Gina Harris 42, 46, 59, 66; Paul Kemp 22, 31, 74; Ian O'Leary 2-3, 7, 10; Roger Phillips 87.